HOME FINANCES for COUPLES

Resolve Money Problems in Marriage and Learn Easy Steps to Manage Family Budget

By Leo Ostapiv

Printed by CreateSpace, An Amazon.com Company.

To my Love:

You inspired me to become proactive in my life.

TABLE OF CONTENTS

Intro

I remember my first date with my wife just like it was yesterday. What a lovely evening!

We went to see Nikolai Gogol's play. I purchased the tickets in advance to make sure we would have good seats. Like any other guy, I wanted our first date to be memorable. After the play, we walked in historical downtown and stopped by one of the upscale restaurants to have dessert with a berry mojito. I readily paid for them so as to impress her. I didn't want the night to end yet, so we went to a nightclub. We got thirsty after too much dancing and decided to grab a couple of drinks. My future wife offered to pay for them, and she did. As I've always wanted a financially independent girlfriend, my thoughts were, "Wow! That's cool; she paid for our drinks. I like her even more."

Money is always somewhere in our brains, even if it's in the subconscious. We carry our own set of financial values with us and, like it or not, the right side of our brain (the rational side) is scanning each potential long-term relationship partner: *"What is his (her) attitude toward savings and spending? What is his (her) earning potential?"*

After all the initial tests are passed, you feel "I found the one! We will spend the rest of our lives together!" The fundamental money issue arises: a structure of the family budget.

Do you merge all accounts, keep two totally independent ones or use a combination of both methods?

Next comes the most important topic. What are the shared goals of your marriage? The shared goals and dreams are among key the factors to lower the risk of a divorce, so we will certainly start with the family glue in Chapter 1. By the way, I am using the term *marriage* more in its spiritual rather than legal meaning in this book.

Chapter 2 outlines recommended structure of home budget and discusses common home budgeting myths. Next you are going to conduct financial values checkup of your relationship and learn about the differences in money perception between men and women. Moreover, we are going to discuss the creation and purpose of Family Financial Board along with behavioral recommendations for each gender.

We want our household budgeting to be as automated, efficient and painless as possible. That's quite a technical field. You can benefit from my experience and other couples' experiences. If you haven't maintained your family budget yet, I am willing to bet the price of this book (price, net of taxes and Amazon commissions, of course :) that you will start managing your finances after reading it. Chapters 4-8 will give you basic financial terms, plenty of budgeting tips and three major techniques of home accounting to choose from.

Chapter 9 discusses common technical and behavioral problems in marriage and provides references to the best online publications on the topic. Finally, Chapter 10 summarizes common sense principles required for financial success and points for mental transformation as shown in the picture.

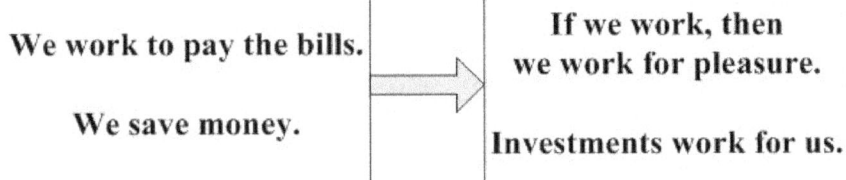

We work to pay the bills.　　　　**If we work, then we work for pleasure.**

We save money.　　　　**Investments work for us.**

It also discusses savings, debt and investments in detail.

Interviews with real couples will show you how they manage the finances and view family financial success.

Finally, after this book was completed and edited, I added the short chapter about technology since it makes our life so much easier. I am a big user of mobile apps, so I felt a lot of my experience will be useful for the readers as well.

Please remember: *Home Finances for Couples* is a powerful tool, not a fiction story for your leisure time. I interviewed dozens of couples, read hundreds of articles from top fifty American and Canadian personal finance bloggers, spent numerous early morning hours thinking and writing to present a truly valuable gift for your marriage!

Whether you are young couple, engaged, newlyweds or you've been together for a long time without serious financial planning, this book will make money something you never argue about.

Discuss chapters with your partner, and use this book to improve your relationship along with your financial health.

Ayn Rand once said, "Money is only a tool. It will take you wherever you wish, but it will not replace you as the driver."

So, take your place behind the wheel and have a pleasant ride with my book.

Chapter 1. Glue for the Family: Shared Goals

Family Glue

Have you ever thought about what keeps a family together? You might name love, positive emotions, personality, chemistry, drive and spirituality. Those things got you into a long-term relationship, but feelings tend to fade after two to four years of marriage. From some point in your relationship, "success in marriage requires falling in love many times, always with the same person."

From my observations, a married couples sticks together because the family glue contains the following elements:

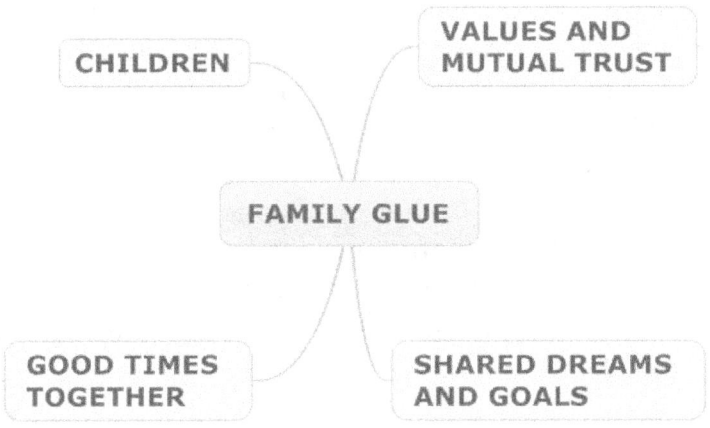

Children are always the Number 1 or Number 2 factor in a couple's life, as stated by numerous researches and surveys. Basically, a relationship consists of two parts: The part before the first baby was born and the part after that. Most parents would agree that by the end of the day, children are a source of joy and the strongest family glue.

Mutual trust and respect require an honest and open atmosphere, where a married couple shares their thoughts and emotions with respect to each other's opinion. We will discuss values and open money talks in Chapter 3.

Good times together are not only memories of your courtship and honeymoon, but also mental pictures of all the memorable moments in shared experiences that happened already or will happen in the future.

Finally, shared dreams and goals are the greatest interest for this particular book, since they are tightly connected with the couple's financial health.

By the way, you might wonder about the difference between a dream and a goal. A dream is usually bigger and more abstract, while a goal has a timeline and is more specific. For instance, a dream is a house in the country with two happy boys playing on the green grass in the yard. On the other hand, a goal is a modern three-bedroom building in the selected residential community with a clear agreed-upon timeline of savings and mortgage plan.

Since this is a book about finance, we are going to be more specific and talk only about financial goals. I split the goals into short-term and long-term categories. Here is a sample list to show the most common ones.

Short-term goals:
- New car
- Major household improvement
- Vacation fund
- Emergency fund (in Ukraine and Russia, it's called "black day fund")
- Health insurance plan with good coverage
- Help for elderly parents

Long-term goals:
- New house
- Children's college fund
- Savings for retirement
- Starting capital for own business
- Financial freedom (money working for you instead of you working for money)

Exercise 1.1: First, please make two individual goal lists with your partner. Select your top three short-term items and top three long-term items from your list. Rank them from 10 to 1, according to importance, with 10 being the most important.

As a real-life example, here is my personal list from June 2013:
- *Short term: Money for birth center program – 10*
- *Short term: Debt free, except the mortgage – 9*
- *Short term: Repaying mortgage – 8*
- *Long term: New house – 10*
- *Long term: Financial freedom – 9*
- *Long term: Children's education fund – 8*

Next, compare your list with your partner and agree on at least one financial goal that your family is going to work on right after the meeting. Also, discuss with your partner 10s and explain why you want to achieve them.

In addition you may take the 9-question quiz to find out how you and your partner stack up against each other — and other people — based on the 4th Fidelity Couples Survey. You'll get tips on what to do next — and their free Couples Conversation Starter Guide.

Money and Happiness

First, I warn you to not overestimate the importance of money. Things that really matter in life are not sold in stores. Love, friendship, family, respect, a place in the community, and a sense of purpose, among other things, cannot be purchased with cash. We've heard this before, but somehow, we give too much importance on money at the expense of everything else.

Researchers (see Angus Deaton's study below) demonstrate that money is a hygienic factor of happiness, the same as health. For example, if a member of your family is seriously ill, your happy feelings are demolished. But it doesn't work the other way around. If your physical health is fine, that won't automatically make you happy.

Second, I'd like to rephrase the cliché: Money can't buy you happiness, but there is certainly a correlation between the two. Let's look at any year of an Organization of Economic Co-Operation and Development (OECD) Satisfaction with Life Index, which measures average self-reported happiness in different nations. You will see the developed countries with high GDP per capita occupying the top positions.

Time magazine published an interesting study by economist Angus Deaton and psychologist Daniel Kahneman, who analyzed the responses of 450,000 Americans polled by Gallup and Healthways in 2008 and 2009. They found that the deep satisfaction you feel about the way your life is going seems to have a benchmark of an annual income of $75,000.

The lower a person's annual income falls below that benchmark, the unhappier he or she feels. But the researchers found that no matter how much more than $75,000 people earned, they didn't report any greater degree of happiness. On the other hand, the happiness benefit of an increasing income is especially powerful among those who don't start with much money, and then the benefit diminishes as wealth increases.

Furthermore, here is a quote on money, voted by Brainyquote.com visitors as among the most popular: "In many instances, marriage vows would be more accurate if the phrase were changed to "Until debt do us part".

Money problems are often cited as the Number 1 cause of divorce in America. It's impossible to calculate the exact percentage as the problems are usually lumped together into one larger cause usually deemed "irreconcilable differences," which basically means that the couple just couldn't get along.

Anyway, according to a recent 2013 study from the University of Kansas, arguments about money are a top predictor of a divorce. Be aware of that risk.

Financial Types of Married Couples

Let us look at home finance from the lenses of a two-dimensional model, where the vertical axis signifies the independent/joint family budget, while the horizontal axis signifies the spending/saving attitude.

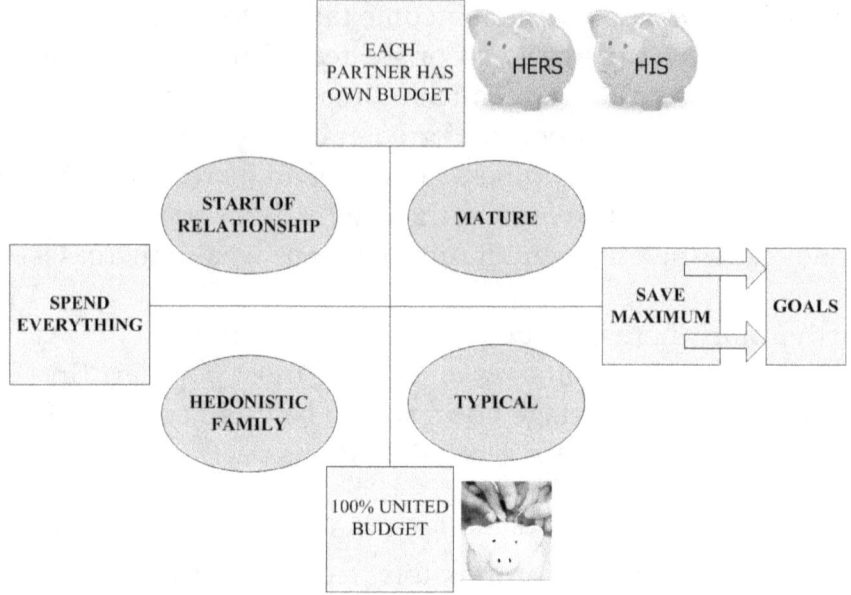

I identify four financial types of couples:

• The first type is the young couple at the start of their relationship: each partner maintains separate accounts and spends almost all the money with no shared goals.

• The second type is the hedonistic family, which combines their accounts, but spends all their cash because of their lifestyle.

• The mature family (third type) is when both partners are breadwinners, and they believe in having their own responsibilities and possess financial self-awareness. They want to achieve some of their long-term goals together, while having personal financial freedom with separate accounts.

• The fourth type is the typical family, which is the largest category. Almost all marriages with one clear breadwinner fall into this category. Also, there are many more families with both partners working, who want to manage their finances together and who are trying to move toward their financial goals. You may suggest adding low-income families with no or little savings to be a fifth financial type of couples in this model, but since spending/saving is more about attitude, most of such families belong to this fourth type (typical).

Let's see what conclusions we can draw from this chart:

Goals are exclusively on the far-right side of the chart. Undoubtedly, partners in a long-lasting marriage must establish a money-saving process.

Speaking of united budget versus two individual budgets, unless you are rich already, separate accounts won't do your marriage any good in the long run. Even the system in which each partner deposits a fixed amount of money every month into the joint account won't be efficient. In my marriage, we applied such a system to our family budget and completely failed. The huge flaw is each partner tends to focus more on own individual account, while keeping the family issues on the back burner. So, while two separate accounts might work for wealthy individuals, they decrease your speed while moving towards financial freedom together.

As you may guess now, I recommend your family merge all home finances and treat money as OURS.

For the sake of clarity, I am not talking about unanimous decision-making on 100% of expenses. Fully joint accounts are a potentially dangerous source of conflict over little "personal happiness" expenses that each person wants to have once in a while. So, I recommend that each partner has a fixed monthly allowance for any personal needs or splurges. I will explain this system in detail in Chapter 2.

Family Money Fitness Program

If you were to accomplish just one thing after reading this chapter, what would you do?

Exercise 1.1 Determine and agree with your partner on, at least, one financial goal to accomplish (together) in the nearest future.

Chapter 2. Reasons to Maintain a Family Budget: How to Structure It and Who Is Responsible

Benefits

Let's get straight to the point. Imagine your total family annual income to be $75,000. You don't maintain a regular family budget, but you still manage to save 10% of your income. That means your actual annual Expenses equal to $67,500 [$75,000 minus Savings ($75,000 *10%=$7,500) = $67,500].

Becoming a driver of your life involves looking at the speedometer, gas level, oil level and all other measurements. You take control of your expenses and become more efficient in controlling them. As a result, you are able to cut unnecessary spending and save more.

Assuming that you live a lean lifestyle already, perhaps you can add an extra 5% toward savings. That gives you $3,375 ($67,500 * 5%) extra savings per year.

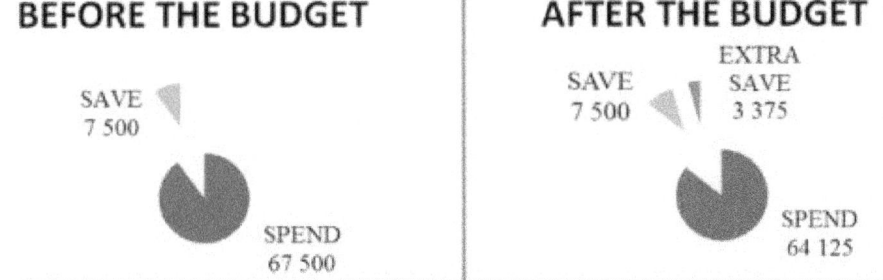

BEFORE THE BUDGET

SAVE
7 500

SPEND
67 500

AFTER THE BUDGET

SAVE
7 500

EXTRA
SAVE
3 375

SPEND
64 125

If you are able to invest that money and end up with 8% yearly return, after 10 years, it becomes a tasty $48,392 in your bank account.

My personal finances are complicated; nevertheless, maintaining the records takes up to a half-hour per week. Let's assume that you are going to become as efficient as I am, so it's 52 weeks * 0.5 hours * 10 years = 260 hours. As a result, you paid yourself ($48,392/260 hours) = $186 per hour for home accounting. Not bad at all and it's tax free ☺

Now, prepare for a horrible secret. Managing the family budget will not increase your incomes in a direct way. That's okay, no worries. What you really need is motivation! Your greatest motive is to move faster as a family, and budgeting is the perfect measuring tool for the dynamics of your income and general welfare.

How to Structure the Family Budget

I have already mentioned in Chapter 1 that the best system is "Ours" money. Let's see how it works, by looking at this chart:

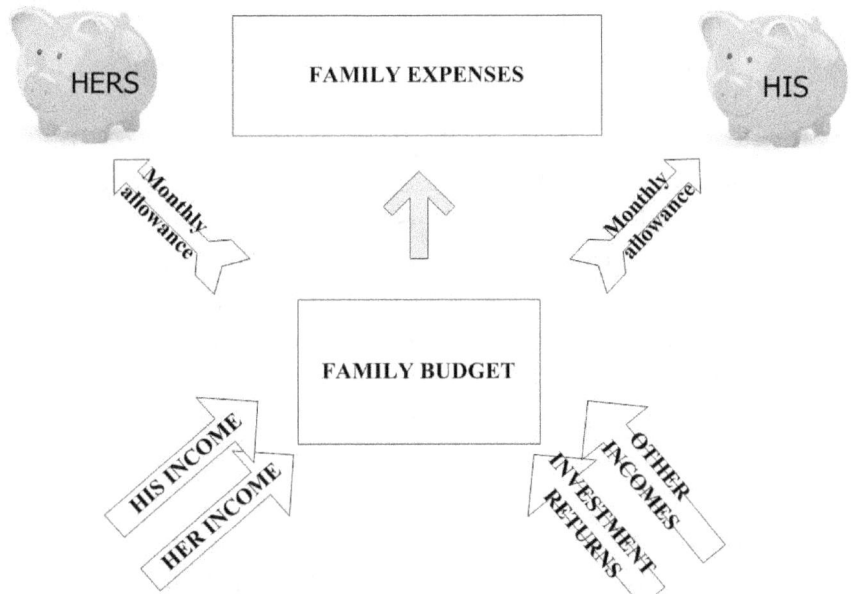

I would recommend having at least two bank accounts for the family budget: a checking account (to which both partners can access) and a savings account. So, you would pay your bills from your checking, while your savings account could serve as an indicator of your progress or emergency fund. It's just a basic set, most of the families have more than two accounts.

In the previous chapter, I mentioned a monthly allowance for each partner. So, how will that work? Here's how.
Some typical expenses for women: personal beauty (hairdresser, cosmetics), non-ordinary clothes and accessories (fancy dress, purse, etc.), hobbies and personal time with friends.
Some typical expenses for men: consumer electronics (smartphones, tablets, devices), sports, hobbies and personal time with friends.

Now, it's time for a short Q&A session:

Why is it so important to have joined bank account? Can't one partner own it, while the other has additional debit card and online access?
By saying "joined," I mean having a transparent account in your personal software, where all the incomes are recorded and can be viewed by both partners.
In terms of legal meaning, joined checking account has benefits (less fees, convenience, might help mortgage, fast access in emergency cases), but they are not extremely important. So the options "primary account holder + additional card" or even two separate bank accounts are up to you.

Is the monthly allowance a fixed amount or a percentage of income?
I'd rather stick with a fixed amount, as it's simple and easy to understand. For instance, agree $800 per month for each partner. Keep it simple.

Should each of us get the same amount of monthly allowance?
Yes, regardless if one earns more than the other. However, if one of the partners specifically asks for less than the agreed amount, then why not?

Do I need a personal bank account for the allowance?
It's up to you. From what I've seen, those who are employed usually have individual cards as well.

How do we distinguish a personal expense from a family expense? Let's say ordinary T-shirts — how would you classify them?
It's up to you, as long as you are going to stick to it. The list is specific for each family; I won't be able to create and enforce a home-accounting standard. Make a list. Introduce amendments and/or corrections within a certain time frame (annually is recommended). The rule of thumb is to have all emotional "little happiness" expenses come from the personal account.

Also, here is a reminder of the purpose of your monthly allowance: It seriously reduces the risk of financial fights over necessary/unnecessary purchases.

By the way, I would treat ordinary T-shirts as a family expense.

Exercise 2.1. Agree on the amount of the monthly allowance for "His" and "Her" needs with your partner.

Who Is the Home Accountant?

Dear Reader, you would be surprised to know that in the families I communicate with, the home accountant position is occupied by men in about 70% of the cases and only 30% are women. That is not a representative sample, of course, and I did not find any general statistics on the topic.

Let's not worry about that. Whether it's the husband or the wife who'll maintain the financial records and prepare report is not the right question to ask. The choice of home accountant depends on personality type.

The classification I like the most discusses four social types of personality: Driver, Analytical, Amiable and Expressive. You can read more about the four social types on Tracom Group's website and take the 10-minute personality test.

Within that framework, the Analytical person is best suited for the position of home accountant, the Driver probably comes second, then Amiable, and the least suitable is Expressive. Even if you prefer some other classifications, let me just point out a few strengths of the Analytical person which you are looking for. Such a person is organized and able to apply a methodical approach to facts and analyses. Besides recording the expenses, the home accountant usually takes care of paying bills and following debt-payment schedules.

FAQ

Isn't it bad if only one person is in charge of home finances?
I did not say that. My point is that one partner takes the primary responsibility of tracking records and monthly analysis, but of course the other one must be onboard and get information at least once per month. You won't survive when only one person knows what's going on.

Myths

Now it's time for the Mythbuster's Show!

Myth: It requires math skills and financial background.
Busted. You don't need superior math and spreadsheet skills to handle your home finances. Modern personal finance software makes it really easy to maintain records and has lots of predefined analytical reports. There is no strict GAHAP (Generally Accepted Home Accounting Principles) to follow.

Myth: It takes too much time.
Busted. Only for a month or two after the start. Once you get the hang of it, and everything becomes more organized, it will eat up only a little of your time. By the way, recording an expense on a smartphone takes up to 10 seconds. Here's a look at my personal example.
Before I got married, I had seven debit cards, three bank accounts in different currencies, special charity account, parents' account, two investment accounts, five types of income and 15 expense categories in my home finances system. As I got used to it, my time investment is less than 30 minutes per week, and I record 90% of the transactions on my mobile phone.

Myth: We are not organized enough, and once we miss expense records, the whole system will crash.

Busted. Psychologists prove that it takes 21 day to create a habit. Read some good books on habit formation. I personally like *The Power of Habit* by Charles Duhigg.

Myth: We only have one breadwinner and little income. Our expenses are paid immediately once we receive our paycheck, so how can this system help us?
Busted. You are exactly the ones who badly need to learn managing your home finances. At first, you take your expenses under control. The more you see where your money is going, the more you can plan your finances and thus, have more opportunities to save. But the main value is coming from the motivation to earn more through financial planning.

Myth: Having a budget means frugality and the refusal of fun things.
Busted. I'd say it means wise spending and setting priorities. There is no automatic ban on dining out. If you can afford it along with your mortgage payment plan, then go for it.

Myth: We have tried a home finance budget, and it did not work.
Contentious. That's a very vague statement, and I don't know the details of your specific situation. I recommend talking to a guy like me to get one-on-one help from an expert.
Result: All tested myths are "Busted," except for the last one, which is "Contentious."

Family Money Fitness Program

If you were to accomplish just one thing after reading this chapter, what would you do?

Exercise 2.1. Agree on the structure of the family budget and determine the amount of monthly allowance for each partner.

Chapter 3. Values to Understand and the Right Ways to Talk About Money with Your Loved One

Values

Some moments in life just burn bright in our memories, in spite of the years that have passed from that very day. Those moments shape individual's thoughts and behavior.

One cloudy autumn day many years ago, I was walking with my good friend Rob on the Rehoboth Beach boardwalk when I spotted a dime on the ground. There were only a few people around, and the place was quiet.
"Are you going to pick it up?" he asked.
"No," I said. "If it had been a quarter, I would have used it to buy a newspaper. However, a dime is not enough."

Rob took it from the ground and looked at it for a few seconds. He looked so thoughtful, and I wondered what was going through his head. He then gave it to me and said, "It's not about the amount, it's about the attitude."

Our attitude makes a difference in just about anything in life. It's what separates mediocrity from greatness, hunger from satisfaction, argument from agreement. Our attitude depends on our values, or what's important to us.

General attitude and perceptions toward money differ according to personality types. Moreover, men and women give different weights to the same financial activities. Many men prioritize entrepreneurship and investing, while women often think in terms of daily savings and stable cash flow. To better understand the differences, let's look at the summary of Prudential's 2012-2013 study "Financial Experience & Behaviors among Women."

	Women	Men
Median income	$51,000	$57,000
Median savings	$12,400	$40,500
Top 3 Financial Priorities	Not become a financial burden to loved ones Maintain lifestyle in retirement Make sure not to outlive savings	Maintain lifestyle in retirement Make sure not to outlive savings Not become a financial burden to loved ones
Top 3 Financial Worries	Household expenses Household debt Saving for retirement	The overall economy Household expenses Saving for retirement
Knowledge of Financial Products	5% Very knowledgeable 49% Somewhat knowledgeable 32% Not very knowledgeable 13% Not at all knowledgeable	14% Very knowledgeable 57% Somewhat knowledgeable 22% Not very knowledgeable 8% Not at all knowledgeable
Current Economic Standing	20% Doing well or 'upscale' 43% Doing OK or 'adequate' 37% Struggling to make ends meet or falling behind on bills	29% Doing well or 'upscale' 37% Doing OK or 'adequate' 34% Struggling to make ends meet or falling behind on bills
Confidence in Financial Decision Making	22% Very well prepared 63% Need help or need to catch up in many areas 15% Are self-described 'beginners'	37% Very well prepared 57% Need help or need to catch up in many areas 7% Are self-described 'beginners'
Risk Tolerance	49% Willing to take a risk for the opportunity of a greater financial reward 22% 'Enjoy' investing	70% Willing to take a risk for the opportunity of a greater financial reward 40% 'Enjoy' investing

How do we know and understand the values of our marriage partner? The best way is to observe and ask the right set of questions. Being in a long-term relationship, you should perform a financial-values diagnosis of your marriage.

1.   Did we honestly open up all personal accounts at the first money discussion? Are there any hidden debts?
2.   What is the individual attitude towards debt, particularly mortgage and credit cards?

3.   Does any partner have chronic financial diseases, like cheating about purchases or not contributing full amount of income?

4.   Do we trust each other and share all personal financial information about potential earnings and planned expenses?

5.   Do we have the same attitude about status symbols? Does a "What do other people think of us?" mentality influence our purchases and our plans?

6.   How are going to cover kids' expenses? Should we have a college education account?

7.   Can we agree on our investment priorities to make money work for us in the future?

For entrepreneurs: Do I have a transparent accounting system to separate business money from the family budget? Do I risk or invest family savings for business purposes without my partner's consent?

I'd never believe that you are in a long-term relationship with all the answers being negative. It's just not possible.

If you have negative answers to about half of the questions, it's a cancer diagnosis for your marriage. There are different types of cancer, so not all is lost. Unfortunately, most of the time, the process is very painful, and the finale is a divorce.

If the negative answers come up to one or two, that is flu. For a healthy relationship, there are pills to take and recommendations to follow. Over the course of a certain amount of time, you cure the disease, and the marriage's immune system becomes stronger.

Please, don't expect a personal finance guy like me to provide step-by-step recommendations on how to choose a partner with similar values. A long-term relationship is too complicated for that, and based upon numerous emotional and rational reasons. The only thing I suggest is to make sure you talk about money early and often so you stick together through thick and thin.

At the early stages of the relationship, you might not feel like opening up and having honest talks about all your financial values since that seems "unromantic". One of the ways I recommend to break the ice is to share childhood memories about saving, spending and the way your parents dealt with money with each other. Or discuss a particular movie like "Wall Street: Money Never Sleeps". Or this book ☺

Any discussion will help to get some sense of your partner's values. The good article on the topic is called "Reader Question: Should You Talk About Finances Before Getting Engaged?" posted at www.iheartbudgets.net

Now, let me share an insight from my marriage, so you can get a sense of the essence of value problems in the family, and the importance of knowing your partner's values.

I am a dreamer, and my wife is a goal-setter. We looked in the same direction, however, without the plan and action steps, we were not moving that way. Thus, it caused a crucial crisis in our marriage. Only when I connected all emotional reasons to the situation that I realized I had to adapt. My wife's perspective suddenly became clear to me, and I planned clear action steps to take...

Values are in the basement foundation of your family's building construction. You need mutual trust and respect to open up and discuss money problems without hesitations and fear of what your partner will say or think. That's the best way to make your marriage stable during storms in the economy and resistant to epidemics of excessive spending and overwhelming debt.

The Right Ways to Talk

It's time to dive into the immense ocean of gender relationships. First of all, as a general recommendation, I suggest two wonderful books that helped me in my life, especially in understanding and expressing my love for my wife better.

The first one is *Men are from Mars, Women are from Venus*, written by John Gray and published in 1992. According to Wikipedia, it sold more than 50 million copies. It talks of the main psychological differences of men and women. I don't remember how many years ago I read it, but I do still apply the major principles I'd learned from the book in my relationship.

The second book is *The 5 Love Languages: The Secret to Love That Lasts*, written by Gary D. Chapman. I discovered this recently, being in a tragic mood because of my marriage problems. It brightened my week and gave me a spark of hope. It helped me realize the actions which my wife appreciates most of all. I realized I need to express my love to her in the way that she would like to receive it.

Now, let's come back to home finances area.

There is always a regular meeting in the usual course of any business partnership, where financial statements and business indicators are discussed. This helps in the assessment of how the business is doing and which direction it is going. The same applies to your marriage. It is extremely important that you hold this meeting regularly. I advise holding Family Financial Board hearings once a month.

Practical tips from real couples:
1.   Set a clear approach.

"We meet once a month to discuss our family budget and monthly results," is a vague approach and with years the tradition falls apart.
Try this instead: "We hold our family financial meeting every first Saturday of the month at 10 in the morning to discuss previous month's finances and future plans. If something comes up, and the time we set is not available, the meeting is automatically rescheduled to Monday at 8 in the evening."

2.   Establish some nice traditions regarding the Financial Board. It could be anything that helps to create a cozy home atmosphere. Here are examples from couples I talked to:
o   Buy seasonal fruits
o   Start the meeting with "my greatest achievement last month was ..."
o   "We always play music from our favorite bands."
o   "Only one person speaks at a time. Whoever speaks has a pen, if you want to say something, take a pen."
o   Having high/low game (this one is actually from the movie *Story of Us*).

Don't go too far with candles and stuff; it's not like you are going to have passionate sex after analyzing expenses :) Not that I am saying it never happens, though).

Recommendations for Both Partners:

1. Be open and honest with your partner. Share your thoughts, feelings and experiences about money issues.

2. Discuss financial role models you admire (friends, parents, entrepreneurs, Mark Zuckerberg, etc.).

3. Don't wait until next month's Family Financial Board meeting if you want to bring a particular problem up. You have casual everyday talks within the family; don't go to bed with a frown in your pocket.

4. Accept your partner's little splurges.
For instance, my wife buys printed books. I wonder about the logical rationale behind that act, since eBooks are 20% to 40% cheaper, and you can buy them within 10 seconds. Does it really bother me, in terms of savings? No, I just wonder. Book expense is little compared to more important things. She feels happier holding a paper book in her hands, and I feel happier when she is happy.

5. (Optional). Find and read about the relationship talk technique by John Gottman, author of the book "What makes love last?". The chapter describing it called "Attunement Made Easy: The Art of Intimate Conversation". The major principles:
- Put your feelings into words (positive and negative emotions)
- Ask open-minded questions
- Follow up with statements that deepen the connection
- Express compassion and empathy

Recommendations for Men

1. Women value income dynamics.

Look at two income trails for the next three years. The first one is $50,000-$50,000-$50,000 per year, the second is $45,000-$50,000-$55,000. The Total is the same: $150,000. Within the first one you can invest the extra $5,000 during the first year and end up having more in "Total + Investment income". Now, guess what most women choose when seeing those figures?

What you earn now is not the only thing that's important. Before your family reaches financial freedom, you need to show progress every year and the amount of effort put forth. Be honest, and say what you are doing to increase your income. What professional training have you taken? Do you have an optimistic plan for next year's earnings? Are there any plans for the next three years?

2. SSS.

It doesn't stand for Social Security System, but you are close. Instead, it's Stability, Safety and Security. Your loved one wants to be sure that the bills will be paid, and the kids' expenses will be covered, no matter what.
This is usually not a big issue in families with two breadwinners. Combined incomes certainly make the expenses much more manageable.

But, if you are an entrepreneur, that changes everything. You have to take into consideration the big picture of your life plus your family's needs when starting a business venture, as you are entering a huge relationship risk zone.

Families with only one breadwinner often face this problem, as well. Share the big picture with your partner. If external circumstances are bad, share it, but show a positive side of events and prove that you are working to improve the situation (which I hope you really are).

Here, you could learn from my own mistakes. This is what happened to me: There were two months in 2013 when my company was going through hard times. We were losing clients, letting people go and even delaying salary payments. A situation like that is enormous pressure for the company's CFO. I was sharing my feelings and thoughts with my partner, describing the situation, and I probably sounded far from optimistic. That certainly created an atmosphere of uncertainty.

As I focused on what was happening in the company, I was not able to assure my wife what I was planning to do to get out of that rut. I did not point out that the new clients and sales leads were of higher quality, and that we started to produce our own software products. And, what's more is that my personal income potential was growing as we were becoming more efficient!

The other important thing is to establish an Emergency Fund, which is an amount equal to three months of your total household expenses. Guys, I know that thoughts about emergency-fund money sitting in a low-interest savings account, or your drawer, might not sound appealing to you, but look at it as a "peace of mind" investment for your loved one (and you!).

3. Men have to earn more than women.
This is a controversial statement, but I would still like to talk about it. You might call me "old school," but looking at my life and the other happy marriages around, I do endorse the above statement regarding low-income families and couples in debt.

As a matter of fact, the study called "Gender Identity and Relative Income within Households," (May 2013) states: "Couples where the wife earns more than the husband are less satisfied with their marriage and are more likely to divorce." Even a strong and financially successful woman wants to relax sometimes, and you are the one to grant her those minutes.

Sure, gender roles are evolving and becoming more sophisticated, but we still go back to our traditional roles at times. Our traditional roles have been ingrained in our genetic makeup for so long that men still have the caveman-hunter instincts and the women have the homemaker instincts.

Recommendations for Women

1. One basic expectation of men that has never changed since the hunter-gatherer society is praise for the meat he brings home. If the results are good, a man expects admiration, at least.
What if "good" is still not enough? You shouldn't say that directly and harshly under any circumstances. Look for a workaround plan. Find special moments to show financial needs. Agree on some specific plans. Show underfinanced categories, if plans are not met.

2. Efforts with no results are a failure in a corporation. As a result, employees don't get promotions or get fired. But wait a minute, your relationship is not a pure business partnership. There are feelings and emotions involved!
The worst thing you can ever say to your husband is, "You're such a loser. I should have never married you." The wonderful words to show your trust and support are, "I married you because I put faith in you. I know you will make it work."

Act as the home spiritual leader during hard times. He needs your love, care and support, as much as you do. Most of all, he wants you to believe in him.

3. It's not only about *What* you say, but rather *How* you say it.

The place, tone of voice, language, eye contact, the way you dressed, a time of the day, his current mood — all of those matter, indeed. I hope that after a certain period of time of living with your husband, you can configure those parameters right. Just please remember this: Never demand anything, it should always sound like asking about his intentions.

Moreover, find the magic key to your soulmate. This can be either sitting on his lap or cooking his favorite dish served in a relaxing atmosphere. Be cautious with that special key; it is only used for important issues. You don't want to risk the locks being changed ☺

Let me show you the recommendations for men and women, visualized with this chart:

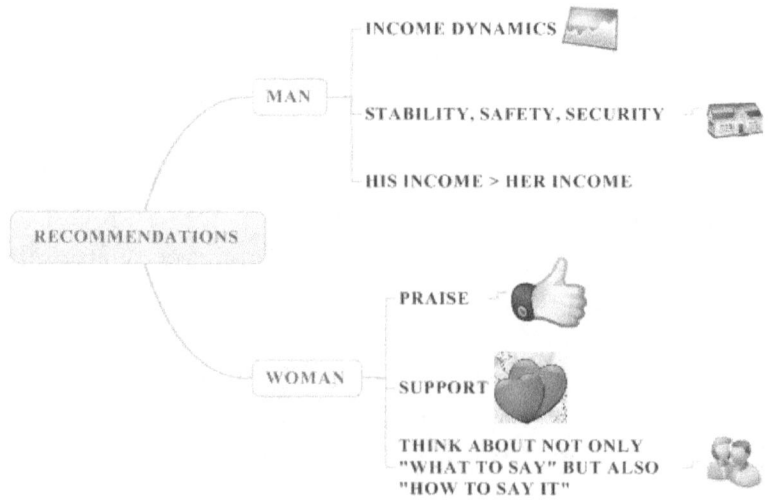

From the chart, it may seem that men are focused on financial responsibilities, while women are emotional partners. However, the right balance of both is the most important thing in modern marriages. Above listed are primary recommendations to understand. At the same time, a husband needs to demonstrate care and support for a hard-working wife, while a woman either pursues her own career or is a stay-at-home mom with some income from her own hobbies.

Q&A

We held our Family Financial Board meeting, and the vote is split 50-50. How do we make a decision?

The methodology that works in the many cases uses following order:
1.   For non-urgent issues, let it settle down for a few days.
2.   Come back to the discussion with new facts and thoughts.
3.   After those two, if it's still 50-50, somebody has to change his/her mind.

Of course, the question is "Who!?" There is no universal answer to that — the answer is whoever feels more like giving in, at that particular moment. If both partners are capable of giving in, then your discussions will be fine in the long run.

One of the best practical solutions I have seen is the "my way" rule. Whenever it comes to a 50-50 vote, you can have it your way. But keep it to strictly one time per month. Your partner gets one "my way" per month, as well. And then, what if it's "my way"' versus "my way"?

D'oh! Then go right back to Step 3.

Family Money Fitness Program

If you were to accomplish just one thing after reading this chapter, what would you do?

Values are the most important; however, you can't learn them instantaneously. It could take months, or even years. So, I suggest agreeing everything about the Financial Board meetings (day of the week, time, creation of atmosphere, necessary preparation, usual agenda, who takes notes, etc.).

Chapter 4. Family Financial Glossary

Before we proceed to the technical side of maintaining a family budget, let's agree on some financial terms. Here they are:

Account: Either a physical account (e.g. your bank account) or your account in the family finance software that has a certain money balance at certain date.

Accrual basis: You record incomes and expenses in a period, when they occur.

Example 1: On July 18, your company promised you a bonus of $10,000 for the first half of 2013. It will be paid at the end of the year. So, you record it as income in July, as if you have already earned it.
Example 2: You paid upfront two months of rent on July 18. The total is $2,000 for August and September. The record is $1,000 in August expenses and $1,000 for September expenses.

Assets: All tangible things you have—money in your bank account, house, car, investments, deposits, patents, copyrights, loans to friends, shares, etc.
For instance, if the individual item has value and can be sold for more than $2,000, I'll treat it as an asset in my own home finances.

Cash basis: You record incomes and expenses when cash inflows and outflows occur.
In the examples above, you record bonuses when they're paid, and the rent expense is $2,000 in July.

Expense: We all know what this is ;)

Incomes: Obviously, this is your incoming cash. In the corporate world, those are called revenues (sales), but for home finances, we use the term "incomes."

Investments: These are part of your assets. Let's agree that, under this term, we mean all money, in some liquid form, that are capable of bringing returns, e.g. savings bank accounts, bonds, stocks, etc.

Liabilities: Your debts, mortgage and different types of loans.

Net assets (Net worth): Total Assets minus Total Liabilities

Net profit (Net savings): Incomes minus Expenses, over the period (month, quarter, year …)

Lou and Oki: An imaginary couple with two breadwinners and two kids; we will meet them in the examples below.

Q&A

If I invested money in self-education, isn't it like acquiring an asset?
Well, you're right about acquiring asset, but it's an intangible one. You can't hold it in your hands, and you can't sell it. It might bring positive effect into your future cash inflows, or might not. Therefore, I recommend recording it as an expense in "Self-education" category.

Do you recommend accrual or cash-basis methodology for home finances?
I have seen couples using either one successfully. Personally, I prefer cash basis, as it is easier to comprehend for both partners and requires less time. You may see particular months' results distorted because of large one-off items, but yearly perspective is usually fine.

Frequency

Also, at this point, I want to introduce a Frequency (of recording) table, which will be explained in detail later on.

Action	Recommended recording frequency
Record cash expense	Within 15 minutes after payment
Bank account (debit card) expense	Once a week
Record income	Within a day of the occurrence
Analyze reports	Once a month before Financial Board
Record non-cash income/expense	Once a year
Financial Board (meeting)	Once a month
Budget groceries and other day-to-day expenses	Give it a try once. If it works for you - continue
Budget vacation and entertainment	Monthly
Budget big purchases	As needed
Family financial health check	Once a year
Plan shared financial goals	As needed

Chapter 5. Basic Technique: Expenses only

"Don't tell me where your priorities are. Show me where you spend your money, and I'll tell you what they are." — James W. Frick

A Few Words about Software

For my home finances, I use the web-based service called Homemoney (http://ihomemoney.com). It has two extremely important advantages: a user-friendly interface and great iPhone/Android versions. Mobile is tremendously important—as I mentioned before, 90% of the expenses I record on my smartphone. Your percent is likely to be lower, but either way, a smartphone helps a lot.

The Kiplinger's web site gives great overview of best personal finance software tools.

Best overall site - Mint

Mint even recommends amount based on your spending history. Your budget bars fill up with each transaction you make; as they approach the limits, they go from green to yellow to red. Free.

Best for Debt Diggers - Ready for Zero
Like most other budgeting sites, you start by linking your
financial accounts. Then you create a debt-repayment plan
based on what you can afford every month or the date you
plan to be debt-free. The site will also show you how much
you'll pay in interest, as well as how much time and money
you'll save compared with making only the minimum
payments. Basic plan is free.

Best for Financial Newbies - Learnvest

With your current budget displayed alongside LearnVest's
optimal budget, you can clearly see where you have room for
improvement. For further financial guidance, you can talk to
an expert -- free. "Financial advice is not a luxury item," says
founder Alexa von Tobel. "It should be available to the
masses." A free financial checkup includes a phone
conversation with a certified financial planner, who will
evaluate your finances and offer some advice on what steps
you can take next.

Best for Over-Spenders - Mvelopes

Mvelopes digitizes this approach to money management with
great success. The site's average user is able to cut spending
by 10%, says chief executive Steve Smith. "You really start
managing your finances instead of just reacting to things that
happen on a monthly basis." With the free membership, you
can link up to four financial accounts.

Best for Game Players - Payoff

If you want to have fun while you work on your financial
goals, try Payoff.com. As with other online money-
management tools, you link your accounts and can view all of
your transactions in one place. But taking the focus off of the

dollars and cents, the site's main attraction is its approach to helping users reach their goals. Free.

My personal addition to the Kiplinger's list - **User friendly site with great mobile apps - <u>YNAB</u>**

Beside great software it offers unique method of managing money (4 rules) + free nine day learning course.

And of course, if you want an easy to start solution - download free household budget template in Excel from my blog <u>http://www.homefinances.info/2013/08/free-household-budget-template.html</u>

Technique Description

The following would be a basic set of your accounts.

Basic technique simplifies everything, so your major task is to record expenses on the cash basis. Every time you pay an expense, a record is made in the system, such as the following:

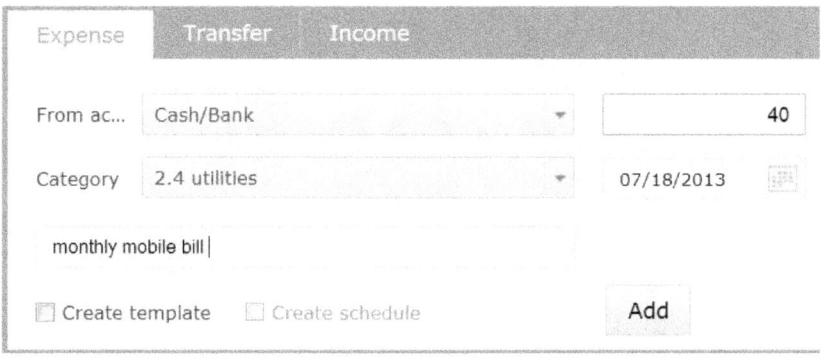

Here is the sample expense categories list from Lou and Oki's family budget:

01 Food

grocery shopping

Lunches etc.

02 Household

2.1 electronics

2.2 home improvments

2.3 rent

2.4 utilities

03 Transport

3.1 gas

3.2 insurance

3.3 maintenance

3.4 public

04 Kids

4.1 kids' stuff

4.2 kids' education

4.3 kids' medical

05 Health&Beauty

    5.1 fitness

    5.2 medical

    5.3 cosmetics

06 Clothing

07 LOU allowance

08 OKI allowance

09 Debt interest

10 Fun

    10.1 dining/movies out

    10.2 vacation

    10.3 gifts/celebrations

    10.4 books. music. movies

11 Parents

12 Self-education

13 Tax

14 Charity

15 Misc

    15.1 bank commissions

    15.2 other

Let me make a few comments on it:

1.   Don't have more than 15 main categories on your list. The optimum amount, for maintenance and future analysis, is between 10 and 15.

2.   As you can see, I added numbers to the categories to establish a structure. It's helpful for viewing analytics. Also, that's a way to keep categories with most transactions on top, but you could use Favorites for that purpose, also.

3.   I strongly warn you not to use a three-level hierarchy by creating sub-categories of sub-categories (Fun -- Purchases of content -- Music). Remember, we want to have a time-

efficient family money-management system; the point is to keep all the work under 30 minutes per week. Keep it simple.

4.   If you feel the need for additional "Other" in any specific main category, feel free to add it. For instance: 10 Fun -- 10.5 Other.

5.   The sub-category 15.2 Misc -- Other is magical; you can use "Other" for anything that doesn't fit the logic of all categories above it.

A sample list of categories is just a skeleton of your own family's list. In your case, it might be that your parents help you financially, so an income category would be "Parents." Or, you want the Kids category to be much more detailed, containing books, gifts, celebrations, trips, etc. Change the list as you wish to make it work for your family!

Recording expenses is about three easy things:

1)   Record cash transactions within 15 minutes after they're completed.

2)   Record bank account and cards expenses at least once a week. Set a weekly reminder on your phone or computer, whichever gadget you are using to record your expenses.

3)   If you have small-business money, never mix them with family budget or use it for personal purchases. Over time, it will create chaos in both systems. The same relates to all types of corporate cards and funds.

Exercise 5.1
Make a report showing each expense category as a percentage of total expenses. Analyze those with your partner. Find at least one category where the percentage seems not right for both of you. Agree on an action plan to change it.

Q&A

Isn't it is a better solution to have, two separate accounts for Cash and Checking in the basic setup?

In fact, I do separate accounts in my home finances. But that requires an internal transfer each time you withdraw money from ATM or deposit to your checking account. Therefore, a joint Cash/Bank should be easier to maintain.

Savings and Debts

You may have noticed other accounts: Debt and Savings. Whenever you repay debt or transfer money to savings (investment) accounts, it is a cash outflow not an expense. So, you have to make an internal transfer within the system:

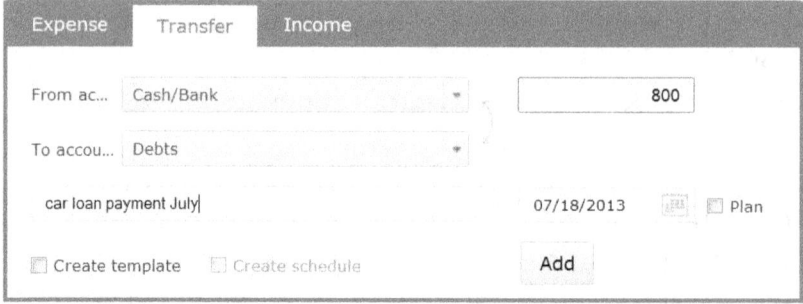

Pros of a Basic Approach

The basic technique is perfect for beginners to form a habit. It gives you a taste and a feel for family-money management. Your first positive results of recording will inspire you to continue.

There's no need to balance Homemoney system accounts with real Cash/Bank, Debt, and Savings accounts, since it's a very basic approach.

Basic approach also allows you to cut unnecessary spending and stimulates saving. The visuals will cause you to reflect on your expenses.
 Examples of good questions to ask:

a.   Why do we spend on category X so much?
b.   Shouldn't the Fun category be less than the percentage Y of all expenses?
c.   Is there anything we can do to increase tax deductions and pay less tax?
d.   Can we afford a second car since the monthly car expense is Y?
e.   How much are we going to save per month, if we start bringing lunch from home? Is it worth it?
f.   We spend Z amount on Kids, which is % of all expenses — how is that aligned with our shared financial goals?
g.   Where does unnecessary spending come from?

With this system, you can always clearly see:
a.   How much debt you repaid over the period
b.   The amount of saved money during the period

Q&A

Can you list a recommended percentage for each category out of total expenses?
I can't, since those depend on the type of your family, priorities you set and goals you want to achieve.

Do I have to register in some online service? Can't I just use Excel for a few months to check how it works?

I recommend using software, but if you want to start with Excel, there is a free template at my blog homefinances.info

Cons of a Basic Approach

While a basic approach is very simple, one major disadvantage is easily noticed: It does not show the big picture.

Another drawback is that you can't actually check yourself. Since you are not balancing accounts, once you miss recording some expense, it's gone forever.

Also, you can't calculate Net Worth.

Family Money Fitness Program

If you were to accomplish just one thing after reading this chapter, what would you do?

For beginners: Make the first step! Register for an account, make a list of categories and start recording expenses. Keep going for AT LEAST a MONTH and analyze the results after that.

To those who already have a family budget: Review your list of categories with your partner. Can you improve it by getting some ideas from this chapter?

Chapter 6. Regular Technique: Incomes and Expenses

"I am indeed rich, since my income is superior to my expenses, and my expense is equal to my wishes." — Edward Gibbon

Technique Description

As you might guess, the regular technique is about recording incomes, along with expenses. Obviously, both a husband and a wife want to know their net savings for each month, so they plan on that.

Let's go back to Lou and Oki's household. Their list of incomes is much shorter and easier to maintain than the expenses list.

1 Lou's salary

2 Oki's salary

3 Lou's other incomes

4 Oki's other incomes

5 Investment returns

6 Bank interest

7 Misc

Lou and Oki's other incomes include the money they make outside the main job. The typical examples include an extra job, freelancing, selling homemade stuff, etc. You can also see that this family intends to invest money and differentiates investment returns with the interest on bank savings accounts.

Once the regular technique is applied, Lou and Oki are able to create a primary report for home finances. It's called an Income Statement, and it shows your household's Net profit.

That's one of key things you need to discuss during your Family Financial Board monthly meetings.

Here is what Lou and Oki's Income Statement looks like:

Income	Jan
1Lou's salary	3,000.00
2Oki's salary	3,000.00
5Investment returns	
7Misc	78.00
Total incomes	6,078.00
Expenses	**Jan**
01Food	1,031.00
grocery shopping	841.00
Lunches etc.	190.00
02Household	1,615.00
2.3 rent	1,400.00
2.4 utilities	215.00
03Transport	170.00
3.1 gas	120.00
3.4 public	50.00
04Kids	931.00
4.1 kids' stuff	331.00
4.2 kids' education	600.00
05Health&Beauty	87.00
5.3 cosmetics	87.00

07 LOU allowance	800.00
08 OKI allowance	800.00
09 Debt interest	
10 Fun	85.00
10.1 dining/movies out	60.00
10.4 books. music. movies.	25.00
Total expenses	**5,519.00**
Expenses/incomes	559.00

As you can see, Lou and Oki's Net Profit (Net Savings) for
January was 559/6078 = 9.2% of monthly income. The typical
question is "How much should we save relative to our
income?"

Many personal finance experts advise 10%, which is fair in my
opinion. The exact number depends on your big-picture goals,
and in many situations, it should be more than 10%. There is
an optimum percentage between spending and savings for
each individual situation.

 I diagnose extremes in spending/savings balance for a typical
family by looking at two indicators:
1)   Savings less than 5%
2)   Not taking into account the investment returns, savings
are more than 50% of monthly income (perhaps, a too frugal
lifestyle)

Savings, Investments and Debts

The regular technique requires you to balance Homemoney
system accounts with real ones. Also, you need at least four
accounts, even in the simplified set.

Upon registration, you record your beginning cash & bank, debt, savings and investment balances in the system. Then perform weekly synchronization of the Homemoney balance with the real Cash/Bank Checking account, and monthly synchronization for the other three accounts.

Net worth ?	559.00 USD
Cash/Bank Checking	0.00 USD
Debts	0.00 USD
Investments	0.00 USD
Savings	559.00 USD
Set up accounts	

As you can see, Lou and Oki transferred their January net income to a Savings account. It might be because they are trying to build an emergency fund.

Q&A

My Homemoney Cash/Bank Checking account doesn't balance with the real one. What do I do with that?
Well, a lot of home accountants face that problem once in a while. In 90% of the cases, it's because the expense record was missing. The rest is caused by omission of some income or a transfer to another account.

You must always trust your real account balance, so your task is to correct Homemoney. I usually check whether my other accounts are all right or not, and then make a technical record into the Misc category, so it corrects the math in Homemoney.

After a few months of recording and analyzing your home finances, such differences will either disappear or become very minor.

Pros

On top of expense analytics, you can analyze the key report of home finances: Income Statement.

Once you have the history in your Homemoney system, you can compare your incomes over historical time period and track your progress in making more money.

You can easily see a percentage of the income you save monthly. Establish a target for your household regarding savings, and make necessary improvements in your spending/saving balance.

Finally, after knowing your actual net profit, you may plan steps and payments schedule toward your financial goals.

Cons

The method requires you to balance Homemoney accounts with your real ones, which could be a hassle sometimes, especially if you have borrowing/lending transactions with your friends and relatives.

But the strongest disadvantage is that you do not see the actual net worth of your household, outlining all assets and liabilities on a certain date.

Family Money Fitness Program

If you were to accomplish just one thing after reading this chapter, what would you do?

Calculate the percentage of your net income relative to your total income for last quarter. Make a forecast to show how long it would take you to reach your first goal from Exercise1.1.

Discuss with your partner whether there are any steps that your family can take to reach the goal faster.

Chapter 7. Advanced Technique: Family Assets, Liabilities and Income Statement

Warning from the Author: Skip this Chapter if you feel the last one was not easy to comprehend.

Technique Description

In the 15th century, Franciscan Friar Luca Pacioili invented a system of double-entry bookkeeping. It's the golden rule of the financial world and the basis for the modern financial-reporting standards. The rule says that each entry has two sides and influences two accounts. It's also called debit and credit side. Regarding home finances, the rule creates the home-accounting equation, which is Net Worth = Assets minus Liabilities.

The advanced technique applies the doubly-entry principle and requires all of your real accounts (including assets) maintained in the system. Let's see how the advanced technique application works, in Lou and Oki's home finances. Their full set of accounts as of February 28, 2013:

Account	Jan USD	Feb USD
Cash	**559.00**	**559.00**
Cash	559.00	559.00
Deposits	**0.00**	**0.00**
Savings Bank 1	0.00	0.00
Savings Bank 2	0.00	0.00
Credits	**0.00**	**-29,700.00**
Car loan	0.00	-27,200.00
Credit Card Bank 1	0.00	-2,500.00
Bank accounts	**0.00**	**1,410.00**
Checking Bank 1	0.00	710.00
Checking Bank 2	0.00	700.00
Contractors	**0.00**	**450.00**
We loaned money to Friends/Family	0.00	450.00
We owe money to Friends&Family	0.00	0.00
Assets	**0.00**	**30,800.00**
Car	0.00	28,000.00
Household electronics	0.00	2,500.00
Investments	0.00	300.00
Total	**559.00**	**3,519.00**

As you can see, their net worth is $3,519 as of end of Feb. It improved from $559 as of January 31, so the family Net savings for February was $2,960, which is $3,519 minus $559.

Exercise 7.1. Using the same logic (assets minus liabilities), calculate the net worth of your family.
Make a list of assets first. Where there is no clear valuation, use your best judgment and the Internet. Debts shouldn't be a problem, right? You know them all.

Besides incomes and expenses, there are a lot of internal transfers that you need to record under this advanced method.

E.g., when you make a regular principal payment on a car loan, it should also be recorded as an internal transfer, while interest is an expense. See the two images below:

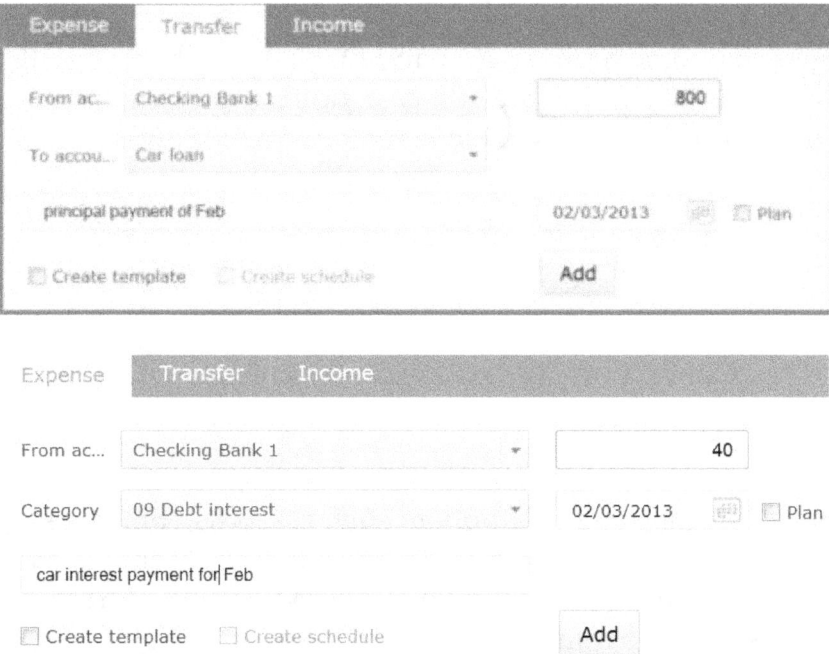

Non-Cash Transactions

So far, everything was relatively easy, since each transaction was either cash outflow or cash inflow. With the advanced technique, it is more complicated because of assets revaluation.

Lou and Oki bought the car for $28,000 in February 2013. Let's imagine it is end of the year, December 31. Obviously, this car costs less. How much less? I do not advocate the use of the depreciation concept in home finances because that is just so complicated.

I suggest evaluating it by using your judgment. If you are going to sell your assets, how much will you be able to sell them for?

Going back to our example, Lou and Oki believe they can sell the car for $25,000, so $3,000 non-cash dollars were lost from their net worth. The transaction is recorded as follows:

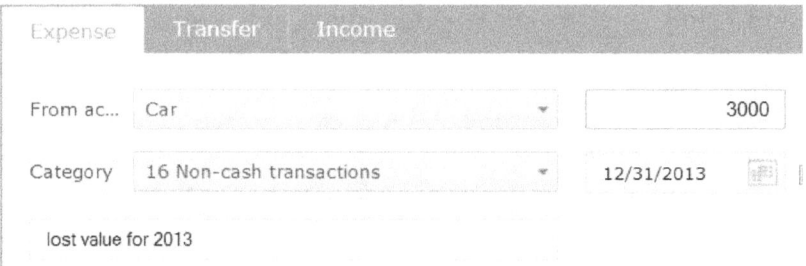

The non-cash transactions apply to such assets as your house, car, household electronics, stocks portfolio, mutual funds, etc. And just to remind you, in my home finance system, I treat electronics, furniture and home improvements, with sales values of at least $2,000 as an asset, as well.

While a car and your electronics usually go only one way (which is to depreciate), your house value and financial investments can either rise or fall. Let's recollect the booming real estate market of 2006 to 2007. At the end of 2006, your house was priced at $180,000, while at the end of 2007, its market price went up to $205,000. The transaction in the Homemoney system is recorded as such:

Expense	Transfer	Income		

To acco...	House	▼	25000
Category	8 Non-cash income	▼	12/31/2007

revaluation 180 000 as of 12/31/06, 205 000 as of 12/31/07

By doing nothing, you got $25,000-plus to your net worth. What a sweet time it was!

Q&A

Which technique do you personally recommend?
For beginners, it's the basic one.
The regular technique is fairly simple to use. It allows you to form the habit of recording your home finances plus gives the necessary background to continue and move up to the advanced technique.
Regarding the advanced technique, it's the best one, if you are able to keep time spent for home accounting under 30 minutes per week on average. If not – use a regular one.

What is the benefit of knowing your Net Worth?
It's the only metric to show the real Financial Health of your family. By comparing the dynamics of Net Worth, you see the progress towards financial freedom. By the way, you may download free Net Worth calculation template from my blog
homefinances.info

How often do I have to record non-cash transactions?
Once per year is the best frequency for non-cash transactions, as they require analytical judgment and could be time-consuming.

Why is there no 401k, or other retirement plans in your sample?

I forgot to add them, in the first place, since they don't exist in my country.
Next, I decided to keep this book easy to understand for international audience, who may not know about 401k plans or IRAs.
But it's a good question, as obviously your pension plan is an asset and must be included in Net Worth, while monthly contributions would be recorded by internal transfers to Assets.

What are the Net Worth benchmarks to compare with?
I have not found any reliable data for the couples. However, there is a good article on the topic "The Average Net Worth For The Above Average Married Couple" at Financial Samurai website.

Can the Net Worth be negative?
Yes, and I've seen such cases. The liabilities outweigh the assets because of large debts. It's unsustainable, and sooner or later, the family improves its net income and repays the debt. Or, in a worst-case scenario, the family declares bankruptcy.

Useful links

Use service called Planwise for modeling 5 and 10 year future plans including big purchases (car, house etc). It's free and extremely easy to use.

Pros

The advanced technique allows you to see the big picture of your family's financial situation because you have balances of all your savings, investments and debts.

It also blocks major mistakes and omissions, since all accounts are interconnected and must be balanced.

Cons

It's the most time-consuming technique.

Users usually need a financial background or deep interest in home finances to maintain all the accounts.

Family Money Fitness Program

If you were to accomplish just one thing after reading this chapter, what would you do?

Exercise 7.1. Calculate your family's Net Worth.

Chapter 8. Tips on Budgeting and Saving Money

"A budget is, telling your money where to go instead of wondering where it went." — John Maxwell

Budgeting

I used to work for the big multinational company with the large budgeting department composed of six employees. These people budgeted absolutely everything down to the number of staples in the office. Numerous budget versions were sent, reviewed, changed, pre-approved and approved. After that, actual results were vigorously compared with the budget plans, and long memos were written on budget/actual differences.

Sadly, somewhere between Excel files and PowerPoint presentations, the vision of the process was totally lost. All other departments were deeply frustrated about the efforts needed for budget preparation and analysis.

The morale of the story: Your household is not a corporation. Use common sense so as not to overbudget and overthink home finances!

I've heard polarized opinions ranging from, "Budgeting is just too time-consuming for us" to, "We budget grocery shopping." Let me summarize the cases and introduce three major approaches to family financial planning:

1. Big scale only

A couple agrees on shared financial goals and understands the amount of money needed to reach the goal.

Financial goals are convenient when you want to work your transactions towards a particular objective. You can add your own goals or use the examples below.

Emergency fund

[Add]

Car

[Add]

Vacations

[Add]

For instance, Lou and Oki want to create an emergency fund of $20,000. Knowing their monthly Net Profit, they decide that the fixed amount of $500 is a realistic amount that they are able to put aside each month.

It will take them 40 months ($20,000 divided by $500 per month) to reach their Emergency Fund goal. Hence, they set their goal and will track its progress each month:

Net worth ? 559.00 USD

Cash/Bank Checking	0.00 USD
Debts	0.00 USD
Investments	0.00 USD
Savings	559.00 USD

Set up accounts

Emergency fund 20,000 USD
3%

No other budgeting entries were created. Of course, it doesn't mean that Lou and Oki are ignoring monthly analyses and don't think about the possibilities to increase their monthly profit. It's just that they tend to make decisions by analyzing actual monthly results without setting budget constraints on expenses in the system.

2. Big scale plus only the controllable expenses

While we want to control all of our expenses, some of them are less controllable than others. For example, you can't *not* buy bread and milk because you've already spent your monthly grocery limit. I suppose the analogy from the corporate world would bring us the terms "fixed costs" and "variable costs."

Hence, in this scenario, "Big scale plus only controllable," Lou and Oki selected only easily controllable categories of expenses for their budgeting.

Using the list of categories from Chapter 5. Basic Technique: Expenses only they are:

07 Lou allowance, 08 Oki allowance, 10 Fun, 11 Parents, 12 Self-Education and 14 Charity.

07 LOU allowance	800 USD
08 OKI allowance	800 USD
10 Fun	150 USD
Add budget for sub-category	
11 Parents	50 USD
12 Self-education	100 USD
14 Charity	50 USD

The most strictly controlled category is usually 10 Fun, especially 10.1 Dining/movies out and 10.2 Vacation. In fact, lots of couples have Vacation as a main category in the lists, not as a sub-category of Fun.

The point of this approach is to set limits on manageable categories, aside from saving for big purchases.

3. Detailed budget

Some families are willing to control expenses tightly, even for less-controllable expense categories, such as Food or Health & Beauty. They invest time into detailed planning and analyze budget/actual differences each month.

The detailed approach usually also includes planning incomes, so a couple can forecast their net income. The sample of detailed budget for Lou and Oki's household is shown below:

Total: 500 USD   Fact: 6,078 USD - 5,519 USD

				Fact
Income	6,000 USD	Create		6,078 USD
✚ Add				
1Lou salary	3,000 USD	✏	✖	3,000 USD
2Oki salary	3,000 USD	✏	✖	3,000 USD
Remaining income				78 USD
				Fact
Expenses	5,500 USD	Create		5,519 USD
✚ Add				
01Food	1,000 USD	✏	✖	1,031 USD
Add budget for sub-category				
02Household	1,600 USD	✏	✖	1,615 USD
Add budget for sub-category				
03Transport	150 USD	✏	✖	170 USD
Add budget for sub-category				
04 Kids	600 USD	✏	✖	931 USD
Add budget for sub-category				
05 Health&Beauty	150 USD	✏	✖	87 USD
Add budget for sub-category				
06 Clothing	50 USD	✏	✖	0 USD
07 LOU allowance	800 USD	✏	✖	800 USD
08 OKI allowance	800 USD	✏	✖	800 USD
10 Fun	150 USD	✏	✖	85 USD
Add budget for sub-category				
11 Parents	50 USD	✏	✖	0 USD
12 Self-education	100 USD	✏	✖	0 USD
14 Charity	50 USD	✏	✖	0 USD

Couples who use this approach try to stay within their total monthly expenses limit. If one category is going to be higher during a certain month, they take action by cutting expenses in another one.

I rarely meet families who go deeper than that and use sub-categories. However, some people do that, particularly in budgeting toys, educational services, health, clothes, etc. within the Kids category.

Q&A

Which budgeting approach do you prefer?

Try the detailed budget including your groceries first. Stick to it if it works for you! If it feels too time consuming, use either one of the other two approaches.

Although I am a financial expert using the advance technique for my home finances, the detailed budgeting approach does not work for me. The cost of time is higher than the benefit from gaining better control.
On a regular basis, I use the big-scale approach, while occasionally I create the targets for Fun and Self-Education to stay within the monthly limits.

By the way, the other reason I have no limits for grocery spending is my belief in healthy food and natural products for family nutrition. I think of it as a long-term investment in health. Perhaps it's also a matter of lifestyle, and not just personal finance.

Please provide links to high-quality online publications on budgeting for couples.

I like case studies from real couples, since they teach the most valuable lessons. For example, you can learn good practical tips from this Canadian-blogging couple who write about budgeting, finance, frugal tips, recipes and more.

Check it out at http://www.canadianbudgetbinder.com. There's a series of 10 blog posts called: *How We Designed Our Budget.*

Savings

"A penny saved is a penny earned." — Benjamin Franklin.

If saving money sounds like something totally new, you'd better start with small goals. Just like you would do a 5K run before running a marathon. Saving for a romantic two-week vacation can be a good start for joined savings. While big goals are fine and admirable, small steps will do the trick to help you stick to accomplishing your goals.

The real savings Benjamin Franklin meant in his above quote comes from funds you invest and make them work for you. We will discuss investments later in this book, as we are going to focus on saving tips in this chapter. Just remember that $20 saved today is worth a lot more in 20 years' time.

I am not going to cover savings tips from A to Z, since you can find hundreds of them by a simple Internet search. In fact, you can download the free eBook called *How to Save Money on Everything* from MoneyNing.com. David Ning shares more than 70 money-saving techniques in version 1.4 of the book. Another good one is from christianpf.com. It's called "25 ways to save your money in 2013".

Below are my personal favorites:
   a.   Savings Tip #1 (by popularity): Make a list for your grocery shopping before going to the supermarket. This will save you from buying things you see displayed prominently and appealingly on the shelves, but you don't really need. Remember the golden rule of shopping: Buy only what you need.

b. If you smoke cigarettes, this is the easiest (and obvious) expense to cut. Many people have radically improved their lives (health-wise and money-wise) by quitting this unhealthy habit.
c. The next easiest cut is alcohol. While moderate use of alcohol is normal, the typical family can save a lot by limiting alcohol consumption, particularly while dining out. Beverages add significantly to your restaurant bill.
d. Use a drawer or jar for change. It won't save you much, but it is neat to have all your coins in one place at home instead of hundreds of different places.
e. Shop online instead of brick and mortar retailer (not applicable to all goods yet).
f. Don't rush to buy a new device when it's first released on the market. More often than not, prices drop a few months after its release.

Exercise 8.1. Read the money-saving tips from David Ning's eBook. Select at least one new saving tip you like and apply it in your household.

My personal list above and the David's eBook are about specific things, although many of them might not be applicable to you. Therefore, let us proceed to more universal things related to the process of saving money. I call them Automate, Play and Visualize.

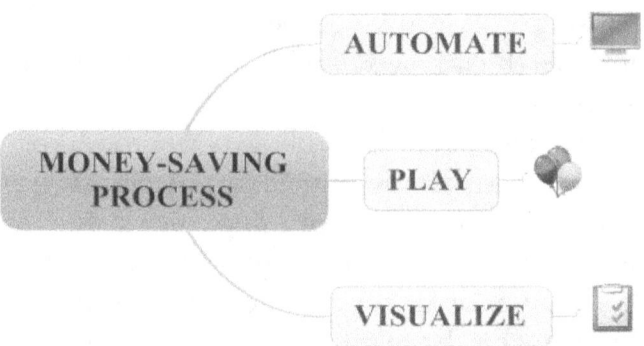

Automate

Readers from North America and the rest of the world would probably have no clue about a Ukrainian bank called PrivatBank. Well, in my view, it is among the top 10 innovative banks in the world.

One of the reasons is because of the ways that PrivatBank offers for automatic online saving. I can create several automatic saving transactions for my checking account online, such as:

- For each deposit to the Checking account, I can send X amount to Savings.
- For each deposit to the Checking account, I can send Y% of deposited money to Savings.
- For each expense from the checking, I can send X amount to Savings.
- For each expense from the checking, I can send a certain % of my spent money to Savings.
- Each month, I can automatically send X dollars to Savings.
- Round up each expense and send cents to Savings.

I am sure you can find similar services with your bank, so introduce modern technology to your saving process.

Play

To break the myth that saving money is boring and painful, let's add some gamification to the process and make saving a lot more fun. Each time you reach a goal, organize a small family celebration. Praise each other!

For the big goals, such as a house or car, you can even celebrate milestones at 25%, 50% and 75% savings rates. Have nice home-cooked meal, a family picnic, do whatever brings your family joy and assurance that you are on the right track.

Many personal-finance software applications give you badges for your achievements, which will encourage you to continue with your progress. Moreover, you can introduce a social element to the money-savings process, if it helps you. In fact, through social networks, friends and family can contribute to your goals, too.

For example, Smartypig.com adds Facebook and Twitter shares to money-saving activity. Another good service for gamification is Payoff.com. It has a cool design and a lot of gamification features to encourage users to do the right things with their money.

Visualize

Use a savings-goal monitor in your home-finance software to track your progress. It will give you a clear visual of where you are in terms of your goals.

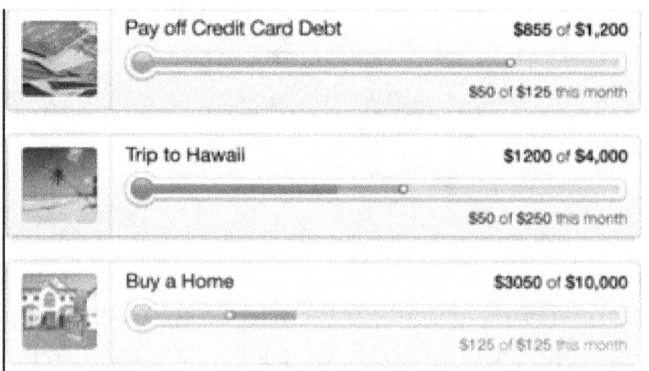

Family Money Fitness Program

If you were to accomplish just one thing after reading this chapter, what would you do?

Budgeting:
Select the approach you like and budget with your partner one month or create one new goal.

Saving:
Choose what you like the most from Automate, Play and Visualize. Plan and accomplish, at least, two actions steps to fulfill it.

Chapter 9. Common Mistakes to Avoid

"You only have to do a very few things right in your life so long as you don't do too many things wrong." — Warren Buffett

Technical Mistakes

I have already shared with you the bad case from my marriage, related to our family budget's structure. As we were maintaining two separate individual accounts, the combined family budget became a secondary in its role.

Also, we were recording family expenses, but not really analyzing them. There were no major decisions made. Such a process caused disappointment between my wife and me. At some point, we'd lost a sense of purpose in recording and creating entries. We felt no value in what we were doing because we were just going through the motions without a clear purpose or direction in mind. Make sure you ANALYZE and DRAW CONCLUSIONS, not just record. Having a complete record is useless if you are not using it to achieve financial freedom or goals.

There are two widely used terms in the global Big 4 auditing firms: "threshold" and "summary of unadjusted differences". Let's adopt them to home finances needs.

For your family budget, threshold is the amount of the minimum transaction. For instance, "I don't create an entry in the software program if the standalone expense is less than a dollar."

I have seen many families using the threshold and writing off the differences to category 15.2 Misc - Other. It's not about cheating your records, but it's all about a goal of efficiency: 0.5 hours per week for home accounting on average.

One more thing: I always round up pennies to save time in recording entries on my smartphone.

The summary of unadjusted differences allows you to not be perfect in your home finances. If your household monthly expense is $5,519, don't scrutinize transactions below $28 (0.5%), looking for mistakes and reclassifications.

When we do grocery shopping in Ukrainian version of Walmart, we usually buy food, as well as gifts, cosmetics, household stuff and sometimes, clothing. If I see that purchases from other categories are substantial, I have to split the check into different categories and make several entries in Homemoney.

But if we buy primarily food, plus a few cosmetics items, it all goes under Food. Yes, I know it's not exact. Most of us are imperfect; we are human after all. If it doesn't distort the big picture of our monthly expenses, then I can live with that.

Exercise 9.1. Analyze how much time you spend monthly on family budgeting, without including the Family Financial Board meeting time.

If the figure is more than four hours, define the most time-consuming activity and ways to do it more efficiently. Research the software available to make you more efficient.

Behavioral

The worst thing to happen in your financial relationship is financial infidelity. If one partner cheats by hiding some important information, it's a dangerous threat to the atmosphere of trust and respect. The ways to deal with it are very delicate.

The following is a bad way to deal with this situation: "My wife went shopping and bought new dresses and handbags out of the family debit card. We agreed that purchases like that should come out of our personal accounts. But since she broke our agreement, I will charge an Xbox and a couple of games on our family debit card." No!

Sliding downward into a spending spiral burns down your home finance system. Never take revenge by reacting to partner's financial misconduct through unplanned purchases. Remember that home finance — and your relationship — is not about one-upmanship. It's about creating a harmonious financial situation for your family.

First of all, there are different levels of misconduct. Buying a new dress is completely different from draining the emergency fund on a trip to Las Vegas. Try to understand the underlying reasons instead of blaming. Discuss how your feelings were hurt, plus forgive minor wrongdoings. Doing exactly the same (financial misconduct) might give you some temporary satisfaction, but it will definitely be a setback for your relationship.

As for major misconduct, such as gambling or shopaholism, I doubt you can solve the problem by yourself. The thing to do is to get a third party to help. It could either be a trusted friend, family counselor or a therapist, depending on the situation. There are some things that we can't handle on our own, and that's when a professional's help is needed.

Compared to financial infidelity, all small family fights over priorities of goals and spending allocation are a normal course of any relationship. What's important is that you talk everything out and find a common ground. You're lucky if you and your partner have the same thoughts about everything, but that's an exception rather than the rule. It's not really about finances that you are dealing with, but values.

Exercise 9.2. If you are having difficulties in agreeing over goals and priorities, please re-read Chapter 3. "Values to Understand and the Right Ways to Talk About Money with Your Loved One" together with your partner.

Useful links

Huffingtonpost Financial Advice For Couples To Avoid Fights About Money
Dinksfinance: 5 Common Mistakes Couples Make when Managing their Money
Studentdebtsurvivor: Spending Without Spouse Approval
Readyforzero: Dealing with Debt as a Couple

Two More Things

First, sometimes I hear extravagant saving advice, like the following: "Always leave small tips when dining out." Well, even being a non-native English speaker, I understand the difference between "frugal" and "mean" pretty well. I hope you do, too, so please don't go to extremes.

Secondly, it's good to have occasional family financial health checkups. The best family doctor ever is your mortgage broker. When you apply for a loan, this person will scrutinize your home finances and life, and then give you the diagnosis. But obviously, you can't go and ask for a mortgage loan each year. The yearly overview of Net Worth dynamics is a recommended way to do the checkup.

It's very beneficial to discuss parts of home finances with friends. Clearly, there is no need to disclose sensitive data about all accounts without your partner's consent.

But sharing experience about techniques and expense budgeting really helps to make managing the family budget more efficient. You might get a tip or two from your friends, which you can apply to your own home finances. And vice versa.

Family Money Fitness Program

If you were to accomplish just one thing after reading this chapter, what would you do?

Find a trusted family friend or relative to discuss financial issues and share experiences. If it's not possible to have one person for both partners, then think about finding an independent professional.

Having two friends, one for the wife and one for the husband, is not a solution, since you have to play on the same team to win.

Chapter 10. Make Your Dreams Come True: Strategies to Make Your Family Financially Successful

"You must gain control over your money, or the lack of it will forever control you." — Dave Ramsey *(popular American financial author, radio host, television personality and motivational speaker).*

I've read a great number of books, publications and blogs on leadership, success and personal finance. They helped me to do many right things in life; however, it did not stop me from committing mistakes.

For a very short period in my 20s, my passive income from stocks was bigger than my full-time job earnings. A few years later, I lost all savings in the stock market crash. Although in the U.S., stocks recovered from the losses in 2010-2013, that recovery never happened here in Ukraine.

We often forget about common sense, like me investing absolutely all savings in highly speculative stocks and waiting for huge returns. But common sense is always there, saying: "Balance your portfolio" and "Invest, not speculate." No need to let the cat out of the bag. You know the common sense already.

Let me summarize everything I've read about financial success into a simple financial model for your life. These are like three underlying principles of the U.S. Constitution, the supreme law of your financial life, determining all other actions and plans.

UNDERLYING PRINCIPLES OF HOME FINANCES

STAY OUT OF BAD DEBTS

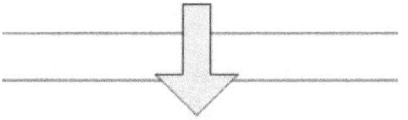

SAVE MONEY

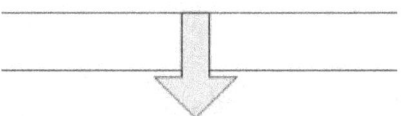

MAKE MONEY WORK FOR YOU

Debt

Enormous debt is the Number 1 problem for the U.S. federal budget at the moment, and it's the Number 1 problem for millions of families across the world. I'd even call it a modern form of slavery for those who are deeply in debt. That's why I fully support folks like Dave Ramsey, who try to educate people and change the attitude toward debt and savings.

Frankly speaking, I have nothing to add to his ideas about debt, except perhaps about student loans.

1. Mortgage: It's okay if it's a fixed-rate loan if you can afford paying it through your foreseeable income.
2. Student loans: This is the only one I disagree about in Dave Ramsey's advice to "pay for education in cash." There are no guarantees of a high-paying job after college, but most of the time, you do need a college degree to get a decent salary. There are a number of grants and scholarships to help you pay your tuition. And, there is always the option to work during college, like I did during my last year.

With all that in mind, I would still take a student loan, if it's a "go or don't go to college" decision. I strongly believe in good education, since it's not only about job prospects, but also about friends, knowledge, alumni networks, opportunities and vital life experience.

3. Car and home electronics loans: Avoid these because no matter how attractive the advertising looks like, at the end of the day, you pay much more than the item's cash price.
4. Credit cards: Let me quote John, a blogger from Frugalrules.com: "Avoid Credit Card Debt Like the Plague." In my opinion, credit-card issuers are legalized bootleggers of the 21st century. Just for the

sake of clarity, I do respect honest bankers. It's just that credit cards create irresponsible spending and consumption, when you are spending money that you don't have yet.

FAQ

What is so bad about using Credit card for rewards and bonuses if I don't use credit money?
Nothing.
In big auditing firms, they say "Substance over form." If you have your own money on your card and use it only for shopping and getting rewards, then it is effectively a Debit card, even though technically, it's called Credit.

I had my personal experience for four years doing that, but the problem was I used credit card for purchases, while covering all the debt by the end of the month. I have not paid any commissions; however, I was living one month in advance of my income. So I finally closed it.

There is a good article at DreamsCashTrue blog: "The smart ways of using credit cards"

Is being debt-free the best decision in terms on low-interest student loans?

To be honest, I have no clear opinion whether it's a right choice to repay the student loan as early as possible. I've never had one.
This question was posted at Newlywedsonabudget.com and there is a controversy around it. Dave Ramsey advocates for being totally debt-free, while many bloggers have a different opinion. Here is a good article about it http://www.doughroller.net/debt/ever-borrow-pay-existing-debt/. You'd better make your own judgment on this one.

Speaking of debt, think about what happened in Ukraine in 2008. Not only did the major economic crisis hit the country with massive layoffs and so on, but the national currency (gryvnya) also depreciated sharply. One week, it was 5 UAH to 1 USD, and the next week, it was 8 UAH to 1 USD. That's a 60% change in a week!

Can you imagine the shock for families, having their mortgages in U.S. currency and salaries in gryvnyas? Suddenly, their debt grew by 60%, along with having a huge uncertainty in economy.

The moral of the story: 1) Take out loans in the currency of your incomes and 2) have a substantial reserve on your mortgage payments. According to Dave Ramsey, your monthly payment should not be more than 25% of family income after taxes.

Savings

During my MBA, we had a class on business strategies. For some reason, the discussion turned to weight loss, diets, healthy nutrition and sports.

I clearly remember how our lecturer shortened the list of weight loss strategies, by saying, "The fundamentals for weight loss are in two simple things: 1) Eat less and 2) Exercise more. Make sure all your other actions align with those two."

How do we apply that to our topic of home finances?

The money-saving strategy is about two things:
  1) Spend Less
  2) Earn More

SPEND LESS — Money-Saving Tips / Do Not Eat a Marshmallow yet / Do Not Keep Up with Joneses

SAVE MONEY

EARN MORE — Be Proactive / Work 2/3 Smart and 1/3 Hard / Earn Extra Income

SPEND LESS

We have already discussed money-saving tips. Therefore, I'd like to talk about the two behavioral characteristics that will help you to spend less: the ability to delay gratification and your attitude toward public opinion.

Delay of Gratification

There is a famous experiment by a Doctor in Psychology Joachim de Posada called "Don't eat the marshmallow yet!" In his study, children were given the marshmallow to eat with the promise that they'd be rewarded with an additional marshmallow if they resisted eating the first one for 15 minutes. Ten years later, the children who held out had grown up to be significantly more successful than those who had eaten their marshmallow immediately.

Successful people know that to get what they really want, they often have to pass on what is offered during the first round. If you can resist immediate gratification or the quick fix, then you will be a happier and more successful person in life. Take a pass on minor satisfactions and say yes to things that will fulfill you in the long run.

The more rationale you have for the big purchase, the better deal you get. That applies to a new smartphone, new TV, new car and, finally, to a new house. Willingness to delay a pleasure for a greater result is a sign of maturity.

Public Opinion and Status (Don't Try to Keep Up with the Joneses)

Often, families find that despite the growing income, the standard of living is also growing with the same speed. As we climb the economic ladder, we often stop appreciating what we've got and focus on things we still don't have. We become used to what we can easily afford and humans as we are, we always aim for something new.

The concept of standard of living is really edgy and debatable. In my opinion, if a two-child family living in a two-bedroom apartment wants a three-bedroom house, that's normal. If the same family got a three-bedroom house, but now wants a larger one like their cousin's, then it's a rat race. Wanting an expensive car, like the one my colleagues drive, is a rat race. An affordable vehicle to make commute trips more convenient is a standard of living.

There is a famous Russian fairytale about an old fisherman and a magical goldfish. The old man caught the goldfish and it turned it was magical. The goldfish could actually talk!

The fisherman let him go without taking the ransom that the goldfish was offering. His wife got so mad and told him to ask for a washtub to replace their old one, which the goldfish granted. The wife gave more and more demands, and grew more proud.

The goldfish got fed up. The wife lost everything she got from the goldfish. All she was left was the old wash-tub she had. You can read the full version of this really famous Pushkin's poetry in English at http://www.barynya.com/tales/fish.htm

The difference between a "want" and a "need" comes down to your lifestyle and the way you perceive the world around you. We have to learn how to differentiate our wants from our needs. This will make us wise spenders. Not only that, but if we upgrade our lifestyle to keep up with our neighbors and friends, we will constantly be on our toes to maintain that lifestyle. To improve the quality of our lives is very different from keeping up with others. There are a number of books to stimulate thinking about your life attitude; the Bible is clearly the first choice.

EARN MORE

Often, the main issue is really about income, not spending; this applies to low-income families especially. Here are the major directions to increase the amount you earn.

Being proactive

Proactivity is defined by Wikipedia as an "anticipatory, change-oriented and self-initiated behavior in situations. Proactive behavior involves acting in advance of a situation, rather than just reacting. It means taking control and making things happen rather than just adjusting to a situation or waiting for something to happen."

According to Stephen Covey, author of the best-seller *The 7 Habits of Highly Effective People,* proactivity is the Number 1 habit that we should develop. It means taking charge of your life, instead of passively waiting for life to happen.

How does it relate to your home finances? Reading this book is part of being proactive with family money. Changing jobs for better conditions and higher job satisfaction is also being proactive.

There are hundreds of websites, books, blogs, seminars to help you become more proactive, but inner motivation is the key.

Work 2/3 smart and 1/3 hard

"Work hard." The more hours you work, the more benefits you receive. That rule comes from the industrial manufacturing economy of the 20th century. But do you know that the service sector was 63.6% and industrial was 30.5% of U.S. 2012 economy output? That's about the proportion for the new rule of the 21st century that "two-thirds are about working smart, one-third is still working hard."

This book was effectively written between 6 and 8 in the morning. I am an early bird, and morning is the time of my highest productivity. So, every single day within a month (including Saturdays and Sundays) I have been getting up at 6 in the morning to write. During these golden morning hours, I've been creating a great number of ideas, structures, analogies and new thoughts. Later, the whole evening was about re-writing, editing, researching information and communication with helpers. Working smart is about the highest productivity for your intellectual efforts.

On the other hand, let me address one myth, called "4-hour workweek. Join new rich." Remember common sense from the beginning of this chapter? It's still here. Getting rich easily by working four hours a week is just too sweet to be true.

Usually, there is a great number of attempts and years of experience behind "getting rich." Malcolm Gladwell, in his famous book *Outliers: The Story of Success,* propagates the "10,000-hour rule" claiming that key success factor is a matter of practicing a specific task for a total of around 10,000 hours. Some people are lucky to invest less hours in success, but there is no magic recipe to cook the fortune.

I am sure you've heard about *Angry Birds.* Do you consider it an overnight success? Here is the story behind. The game was created by Finnish video-game developer Rovio Entertainment, which was close to bankruptcy early in 2009. They had developed 51 titles and were on the market for four years before their huge success of *Angry Birds.*

When I hear amazing success stories about appillionaires and self-published authors, I know most of the times it wasn't just one shot to hit the target. Consider the following statistics. My company Stanfy has been in mobile development since 2008. We've created more than 10 software products, most of them dead by now. None has become financially viable. Only one mobile application has a foreseeable potential to be there as of August 2013.

Earn Extra Income

Look at me. I am writing a book in Kyiv, Ukraine, set to be published and sold at Amazon, Smashwords, Google Play and iBooks. I enjoy blogging, structuring my knowledge in writing and sharing valuable advice with people.

Look around. There are thousands of people making decent money out of their hobbies. There are travelers blogging about their trips. There are housewives sharing culinary adventures and expertise online. There are many writers and editors freelancing online at oDesk and Elance. Also, there are craft lovers selling handmade accessories through e-stores, such as Etsy. There are a number of things you and your spouse can do to increase family income. Just know what you are creative at and market your skills.

Exercise 10.1. Hold a brainstorming session with your wife (or husband) about ways to earn extra profit for the family.
Just to remind you, during this brainstorming session, don't criticize ideas right away. The right way to go about this session is to make a list of all ideas, including the crazy ones. Select one or two ideas that you both view as doable. Bear in mind that the success of your home finances depends on the cooperation of both partners.

Finally, if the debt situation is bad, there is also the option of getting a second job. I had that experience for a few months in my 20s and I consider it too risky for healthy relationships. However if your financial situation is really tough, then it may have to become a real option.

Sometimes, sacrifices really have to be made. As Eric Williams wrote in his book "It's your money: what will you do with it?" – "I was missing out on the friend's party so I don't have to miss out on our own kids' birthdays in the future."

Investments

So far, this book is about how to generate savings while being on the same page with your partner. But the ultimate goal of your family is financial freedom, which requires making money work for you. After that money is a tireless worker. With no vacations or sick leaves, it works 24/7.

I can't go on about investments in detail, as it might take us another hundred pages. Nevertheless, let me point out important steps needed for a couple to start the personal-investment journey.

First of all, both partners should take a 5-minute test to determine the kind of investor they are. You can find it at http://www.dummies.com/how-to/content/what-type-of-investor-are-you.html

Google a good article on investment disagreements and the way to deal with them, it's called: *Relationship Chronicles: How to Deal With a Partner's Risky Investment Choice*

Generally speaking, your family-investing options are within the following traditional investment categories:

I don't have any pension plans (401k, Roth 401k, Roth IRA, TFSA, RRSP) listed on the chart because:
a) you can't get them in every country and b) if you can get one, do it for tax benefits anyway. And just to note, people who live in the United States and Canada are really lucky to have many retirement options, since there are no individual pension accounts in my country. The only singular option we have here in Ukraine is a collective state fund, which is leftover from the communist era.

The "own business" option stands out to a certain point, since it's often not only about the money and returns. I work with small businesses as a consultant, so I've seen many small-business owners making less money than in the corporate world, but enjoying their work a lot more. Again, since this is a book on home finances, let's not divert the discussion to the entrepreneurial way of life. I am just giving you a glimpse of your options.

Finally, besides those listed at the chart, there are alternative investments, such as gold, hedge funds, commodities, venture capital funds, financial derivatives, etc. The rule of thumb you should follow: "Don't understand them? Don't touch them!" But the flip side of the coin is that you can educate yourself.

Dave Ramsey strongly advocates that mutual funds are the best investing option, but I would say that although they are trustworthy, mutual funds are not the only option available. The best advice I can say is to find a professional to help you structure the investments, if you are not an expert yourself.

Before we leave the topic of investment, I would like to emphasize that in investments, the higher the risk, the higher the return. In the chart above, bank deposits give you the least return, but they are also the least risky.

Q&A

Why did you not say anything about charitable giving in your book?

I do believe that giving is very important, and it brings incredible satisfaction returns to givers. I have never been able to reach 10% charity donations out of my income.

However, I worked pro bono as vice-president of finance for one non-governmental organization (NGO) and volunteered at different events with other NGOs. In terms of efforts, I pay charity contributions, which makes me happier indeed.

Once I secure the capability to help charities financially, I'll follow the 10% rule. Why 10%? The figure originates from religion, and I know several wealthy people use it as an indicator.

Exercise 10.2. Discuss charity contributions with your partner, as even a small amount will bring you a lot of moral pleasure and satisfaction. If you can't help financially, there are always volunteer tasks in your community.

What about an education fund for the children, it's not on your investment chart?

As a matter of fact, a lot of parents view good education for their children as primary long-term investment. I neither object nor support the attitude. The investments and returns I structured in the book are within the strategy of "making money work for you."

Is there a step-by-step plan to family financial success?

I showed you the road: STAY OUT OF BAD DEBTS -- SAVE MONEY -- MAKE MONEY WORK FOR YOU. Or, as Rob from doughroller.net puts it, "Make more, spend less, invest the rest."

The speed (monthly net profit), the type of your vehicle (full-time job, own business, additional income, number of breadwinners), and milestones (family financial goals) are individual to your marriage or relationship. Just go on.

But always be mindful of the road signs to make sure that you are still on track. Always have a roadmap and always check in with your partner to make sure that both of you are still going the same direction.

The closest thing to a good detailed plan for getting out of debt is *Total Money Makeover* by Dave Ramsey. Regarding savings and investments, you may check my top personal finance books list at Goodreads. Also, I regularly read some decent personal finance blogs describing real life cases and author's steps to financial freedom.

Another great option is the personalized financial planning service.

The first one is called LearnVest. It offers a seven-step program that takes you from cutting expenses to investing your money. All users get help from a certified financial planner, who has gone through special training and is prepared to deal with many different financial situations.

The second one is You Need a Budget, which offers software, along with the own methodology of four basic rules and educational classes. You also need to know that, while they offer free trials, both LearnVest and You Need A Budget are not free.

Let me quote Dave Ramsey one more time: "What to do isn't the problem; doing it is."

Family Money Fitness Program

If you were to accomplish just one thing after reading this chapter, what would you do?

If you have debts, then make a clear "getting rid of debts" timeline.

If you are free of debt, take an investment test and discuss investment options with your partner. You and your partner have to agree on the investment priorities of the family.

Interviews

I held a number of interviews with couples while working on the book. Home money is a very sensitive and private topic. As I live in Ukraine, I was able to connect only with immigrants from Ukraine and Russia, who live in USA or Canada.

The main thing to learn from Ukrainian and Russian immigrants is their wise attitude to debt and ability to save money despite of income stream fluctuations.

Below are the most interesting conversations.

Nick and Julia, Canada

How long have you been together?
For 7 years already. Julia is better in tracking that :)

How many breadwinners are there in the family?
Nicks has a full-time job, and Julia stays at home with our son.

What is the range of your annual household income?
Up to $75,000 per year.

How many of Dave Ramsey's baby steps have you accomplished in your marriage?
We are not that familiar with Dave Ramsey's ideas, but we do have an emergency fund to cover more than three months' worth of expenses. We have always been very cautious about debt, so we are debt-free at the moment. Regarding steps 4 (*15% of income to retirement plans*) and 5 (*college funding for children*), we are thinking about RESP. (*Registered Education Savings Plan is an education savings plan in Canada that is registered with the government.*)

What is your attitude towards managing the family budget?
Julia takes care of the records and planning using MS Excel.
We have fixed monthly expenses like rent, car, and insurance.
The second part is grocery shopping. Finally, the third amount
is everything else – fun, trips, clothing, gifts, etc., where we
are trying to stay within a certain limit each month. The total
number of expense categories is 16, but we want to merge
some categories in the future. Also, we do make some savings
each month.

*Have you noticed any benefits of having a budget compared to the
times when you didn't maintain one?*
Yes, the first thing is that we clearly understand our spending
and where our money goes. It's easier for us to plan for big
purchases. Budget removed uncomfortable feelings for car
repairs, since we planned some money for that. By the way,
we concluded from the data analyses that repairs expense is
too big, so it makes sense to get a newer car; it's our short-
term financial goal.

What is your usual way of discussing the family budget?
We had many talks before starting it, since Nick had some
doubts about the idea. But at some point, he felt the need to
control our expenses better. Now, Julia makes records every
day, while we have small discussions about planning a few
times per week.

What is your most memorable disagreement about spending?
It happens from time to time, but we cannot remember really
big fights. Our method is to come back for a second round of
discussion if we can't make a decision. We always find a way
to compromise. The last disagreement issue was about the
massage chair for our car. Eventually we bought it, but it
broke after three days. So we returned it to the retailer and got
our money back.

How do you describe the financial success of a family?
First of all, the couple must have savings. We think of additional education for Julia now and mortgage. A financially successful family can afford those.

In general, the income should be enough to cover all living expenses along with the possibility to make savings. And vacations! Oh, yes, vacation trips at least two weeks per year plus weekend trips.

Pavel and Anna, Ukraine

How long have you been together?
For 12 years.

How many breadwinners are there in the family? How many kids do you have?
Two breadwinners and no kids.

What is the range of your annual household income?
Up to $75,000 per year.

How many of Dave Ramsey's baby steps have you accomplished in your marriage?
We are debt-free and have the emergency fund. We try to follow the 10% savings rule.

What is your attitude towards managing the family budget?
We use software, where special accounts "Pavel" and "Anna" have been created. Each of us records personal expenses using those accounts. The same rule applies to all family cards and accounts; whoever spends the money makes an entry in the system.

Once a month, we analyze the picture by going over each expense category. We had budgeting before, but it wasn't helpful. So, we just look at figures and draw conclusions on actual data nowadays.

Why wasn't budgeting helpful?
There is no safe-to-spend balance in our mobile software, so basically, budget limits were useless for blocking the payment at the time of purchase.
For example, you have limit of $100 a month for Health&Beauty, and you know it at the beginning of the month. But it's hard to track how much you've already spent, let's say, on the 15th, 20th, 25th because there is no info on my mobile phone. So you just make the purchase anyway.
And overall, budgeting was not a pleasant procedure for Anna.

What is your usual way of discussing the family budget?
The monthly meeting is at the beginning of each month. Anna cooks dinner, while Pavel does the number crunching. ☺ He tells the results and proposes actions while we talk during the process.

What is your most memorable disagreement about spending?
We don't remember anything big, as buying a toaster is not a big deal. During our budgeting era, we had a situation when Anna was playing with the expenses, trying to record new dresses she bought in different categories. But she hasn't gotten beyond the total limit, and Pavel encouraged her to show and record the real situation.

Tell me more about your financial goals more.
Well, we don't have any big goals like buying the apartment. In fact, "own vs rent" is our major disagreement over family goals. So far, we both agreed that it is the right thing to save money, but we haven't come to a decision yet about what the next big purchase is going to be.

Did you feel any changes in your spending habits after you started budgeting?
It certainly helps to be more cautious. Pasha still keeps a hand-written notebook from old times, which helped to straighten home finances many years ago.

How do you describe the financial success of a family?
When you can buy all you need and money is not an issue. For instance, we have successful friends who own very nice and comfortable apartment and travel a lot. That's an indicator of success.

Ruslan and Anna, USA

How long have you been together?
We have been married for nine years.

How many breadwinners are there in the family? How many kids do you have?
Ruslan is employed, while Anna is studying at university and has no job at the moment. We have no kids.

What is your annual household income?
It's in the range $75,000 – 150 000.

How many of Dave Ramsey's baby steps have you accomplished in your marriage?

We have student loans, a car loan, and a mortgage. At the same time, we have an emergency fund, and Ruslan makes regular retirement fund contributions.

What is your attitude towards managing the family budget?
Income comes to our joint account. Ruslan is our home accountant, who controls home finances. It includes paying the bills, analyzing expenses, monitoring of our bank balances, and planning.
He manages all figures in MS Excel file. One tab is for incomes and account balances. He calculates monthly expenses as "opening balance plus incomes minus closing balance" on the first Excel tab.

The second Excel tab has a list of fixed costs like mortgage, cable, phone, etc. So the "All the rest" expense equals "Total monthly expense from the Tab 1 minus Fixed payments." The amount and dynamics of "All the rest" is the main issue usually discussed within family financial talks.

Even though we only have one breadwinner at the moment, we decided that each of us should have the allowance for private expenses. Our solution is Anna's special credit card that only she can access.

Why don't you track all expenses?
Ruslan used to track every single purchase and knew his monthly coffee expense. But it's complicated and time consuming, so he has come to a conclusion that time investment is higher than the benefit from that information.

We don't have excessive entertainment budgets and understand our "All the rest" costs structure, so there is no value of knowing the exact amount spent for restaurants or movies.

What are the main benefits of having a family budget for you?
It's very easy to compare situations of chaos and order. Last Christmas, Ruslan got very busy and have not maintained data in Excel for a few months. He immediately felt a lack of control and found problems with planning. You immediately start appreciating the order, once you are in chaos. You sleep better if you are able to control your money ☺

What is your usual way of discussing the family budget?
It's a very delicate discussion at the moment, since we have one breadwinner. We usually discuss our planned big purchases and what adjustments we need to make with private expenses in order to save the required amount. Once a decision has been made, Ruslan takes control so that our savings goal will be achieved. It feels like sports sometimes ☺

What is your most memorable disagreement about spending?
Partners usually help each other to make purchases more rational and less emotional. For instance, Ruslan dreamed to buy a motorbike one time, but the question "Do really need it?" helped him to avoid that purchase. Openness is the most important factor to resolve the money issues successfully.

Does debt make money a very sensitive issue in a relationship?
We migrated from a country with a very different debt culture and it doesn't feel natural for us to have all those loans. It creates the pressure and a risk factor in the marriage. The only tolerable debt is mortgage.

How do you describe the financial success of the family?
It's not about the exact amount of money the successful family must have. The level of comfort with what you have is the essence. If you wake up in the morning with no headaches about money problems, it's an indicator of success.

Nick and Olga, USA

How long have you been together?
For eight years.

How many breadwinners are there in the family? How many kids do you have?
Two breadwinners. We have one child, a girl.

What is your annual household income?
It's up to $75,000.

How many of Dave Ramsey's baby steps have you accomplished in your marriage?
We still have the mortgage and no investments. We repaid student loan recently and we have college fund.

What is your attitude towards managing the family budget?
Nick does all home accounting using personal finance software. We have very few cash expenses, so he can download all information about purchases from bank cards. We treat family money as "ours" and all information is open for both partners. Occasionally we discuss the reports together and draw the conclusions.

Tell me more about your financial goals planning.
We have had only one breadwinner for the last four years, since Olga has been studying in medical school. It was tough for us to make any savings because of repaying student loan and contributing to the college fund. The only goal we were able to establish and achieve was $50 from each paycheck to savings account.

Did you feel any changes in your spending habits after you started budgeting?

Before the budget we were trying to keep the receipts and bank statements, looking for the answer to the question "Where did the money go?" It was a terrible mess. Using software makes it so much easier. We clearly see major monthly expenses by categories and control unnecessary spending.

How do you describe the financial success of the family?
It's when your incomes are sufficient to make retirement fund contributions, and at the same, you bear the living costs and can afford travelling.

Vitaliy and Alla, Canada

How long have you been together?
Since 1997.

How many breadwinners are there in the family? How many kids do you have?
Vitaliy has a full-time job, while Alla is a stay-at-home mom. She has incomes from sidelines occasionally. We have one daughter.

What is your annual household income?
It's in the range $75,000 – $150,000.

How many of Dave Ramsey's have you accomplished in your marriage?
We are debt free and we do have the emergency fund. Vitaliy makes retirement contributions matched by the employer and we save $100 for the college fund each month.

What is your attitude towards managing the family budget?

Our family budget is unified, we track every single purchase down to the cents. Vitaliy inputs all the entries into our software program called Homemoney. If Alla buys something, she keeps the check to hand it to Vitaliy. Alla also compares prices from different retailers to get the best deal for good quality products.

There are no separate categories for personal "pocket expenses," they are all within the general family budget. We have dynamic planning and we review our yearly forecasts regularly.

What is your usual way of discussing the family budget?
Vitaliy performs analysis after the month ends. Then we discuss budget/actual differences and the big picture of our financial situation.

What is your most memorable disagreement about spending?
We have similar values regarding money, and we are both financially savvy. We have been together for a long time and have been in different money situations. We had been a family of two breadwinners, a family when Alla was making more than Vitaliy, and now, Vitaliy is the major breadwinner. So we are experienced in finding compromises and taking family decisions together.

Both husband and wife must be on board, it's a key to successful management of home money.

Can you recollect any funny stories related to your home finances?
Vitaliy once mismanaged the checking account and Alla's card by omitting rewards. As a result, we had a really nice surprise when we discovered a decent amount of extra dollars at our account. It was really cool!

What are the main benefits of having a family budget for you?

We started making records and planning a few months before our wedding because we had a goal of fully financing the celebration on our own. We quickly recognized the value of controlling our money after we had started it.

We feel more secure in being able to predict next month expenses. Budget is also an archive log of all big purchases and trips taken, where we can always find historic data for planning.

How do you describe the financial success of a family?
Vitaliy: To get what you want without incurring debts.
Alla: A feeling of internal comfort about the family's money situation.

Andrew and Natasha, USA

How long have you been together?
For more than 10 years.

How many breadwinners are there in the family? How many kids do you have?
We have two breadwinners and no children.

What is your annual household income?
It is $150,000+ per year.

How many of Dave Ramsey's baby steps have you accomplished in your marriage?
First four steps and we also have investments.

What is your attitude towards managing the family budget?

Andrew manages family finances by using Quicken.
Everything is in one place. Most transactions are non-cash, so
you can get a clear picture by importing data from the bank.
Andrew imports transactions once per month and we hold a
family financial discussion based on the reports.

What benefits did budgeting bring to your family?
When you don't budget at all, you don't know what's going
on. There are some expenses you consider small, but the truth
is that they are not. So it's a discovery to reduce costs through
budgeting.

But of course, there are some important things for your
personal happiness you can afford to continue, like Starbucks
coffee in the morning. Maintaining the budget changes human
spending habits to some extent, but not fundamentally.

How do you describe the financial success of the family?
First of all, the financially successful family makes more
money than they spend each month. They are investing extra
cash flow in order to be prepared for storms in economy. The
ultimate goal is to become totally independent of job's salary
because of passive income.

Summary:

When speaking about the financial success of the family, nobody names the exact amount in dollars. There's no exact amount that once reached, a family can consider themselves as financially successful. Couples think of financial success as an ability to afford what you want and internal comfort about family money.

Therefore, financial success is not measurable by the amount in dollars, but by the level of the quality of life.

All couples recognize the value of maintaining the family budget. It disciplines spending, enhances responsibility and helps the couple to sail in the same boat. The top advantages named are feeling of control and ability to make financial planning.

SUPER SUMMARY

One of Dave Ramsey's famous rules is that personal finance is 80% behavior and 20% head knowledge. I have seen that it really works in a number of families, no matter the circumstances.

There are always a lot of excuses to find: financial crisis, bad boss, no luck, stiff competition.

But the underlying question is whether EXTERNAL FORCES DRIVE YOUR LIFE or DO YOU?

Think about your family life and the values of your partner.

WHAT ARE YOUR GOALS as a COUPLE? Is there anything you want to change about your family's lifestyle?

Go to your soulmate and give a nice hug.

Ask, "Are you happy with our family life? Is there anything you want to add about our shared financial goals?"

Listen.

Understand.

ACT!!!

About the Author

August 22, 2012, was my 30th birthday. My wife and I went to Odessa, Ukraine, for the weekend to celebrate and had a lovely time there. The next day, I thought, "Look at me, I am a happy person. What else do I need in life?"

That's how my new dream was born. I said to myself, "Produce some intellectual product (IP) to share with people!" As you are now reading my book, you can confirm that is being achieved.

In 2005, I started my financial career as an auditor in Deloitte & Touche. Since then, I have worked in different positions related to corporate financial management. Currently, I am CFO of a mobile software company "Stanfy" and an independent consultant on managerial finance for small businesses.

In 2003, I got my bachelor's degree in Economics from Kyiv-Mohyla University (Ukraine), and in 2011, I finished my self-financed MBA. Also, I passed all exams given by the Association of Certified Chartered Accountants (ACCA), a global body for professional accountants, and qualified for their membership in 2009.

My personal-finance journey began when I started recording the expenses in Microsoft Excel in 2008. The underlying reason was to discover why I had a decent salary, modest lifestyle and yet neither assets nor savings.

Over the years, I developed an advanced system with the usage of online financial software and regular financial health checks. I invented tricks and techniques to make managing my own money as easy as possible. Hence, people started asking me for advice in managing their money.

At this point, you might think that my marriage gained from a good system of managing the family budget. Nope!

While we established a technically advanced system with lots of accounts, I was blind to the real values of my partner. For instance, my priorities were vacations while we had giant mortgage repayments. We had vague family financial goals that caused disbelief and resentment. It happened mostly because of lack of communication and a misguided notion of "my own" vs. "our" money.

"Fool learns from his own mistakes. The wise man learns from the mistakes of others."

I've done my best to share with you my knowledge and tips on family money management.

Use this book to improve your relationship, your finances and your life!

Leo Ostapiv, Kyiv, Ukraine

P.S. One last thing: I ask you to express your opinion about this book and share your review. In fact, I beg you not to postpone or skip it. The success of my writing is a matter of life and death for my relationship as of August 2013.

PLEASE POST A REVIEW. I will deeply appreciate it.

THANK YOU so much for doing that!

Bonus Chapter "How a Smartphone Can Improve Your Home finances"

Mobile phones have brought tremendous changes to our behavior and our social interactions for the last five years. It is often called the Third Screen revolution after the TV (first) and PC (second).

A wealth of financial apps on the market gives you numerous opportunities to be responsible with your home finances and manage your budget efficiently. You can read reviews of best apps on the web, so I'd rather share my own practical experience and talk about the future.

How the Smartphone Helps Me on a Day-to-Day Basis

I have both an Android phone and an iPhone, so I use both Homemoney mobile apps primarily for three purposes.

First of all, I check my balances and gain confidence about significant unplanned spending (e.g. purchasing a conference ticket), if my monthly spending is normal. Sometimes, it stops impulse buying, especially regarding entertainment.

Second, as I have already told you, I record 90% of my transactions on my mobile phone. Even though I can synchronize my checking accounts once a week with my bank automatically, I can record some debit card payments and incomes on my mobile earlier than that to see the current status anytime.

Finally, sometimes I input bills due into Homemoney using my computer, and I can check on my smartphone when I have to pay them.

I'm also an active user of a local banking app called Privat24. My most common transactions include checking balances, sending money to mom, exchanging currencies and searching for my bank's nearest ATM. But there is a lot more you can do with a decent banking app; just look at this screen:

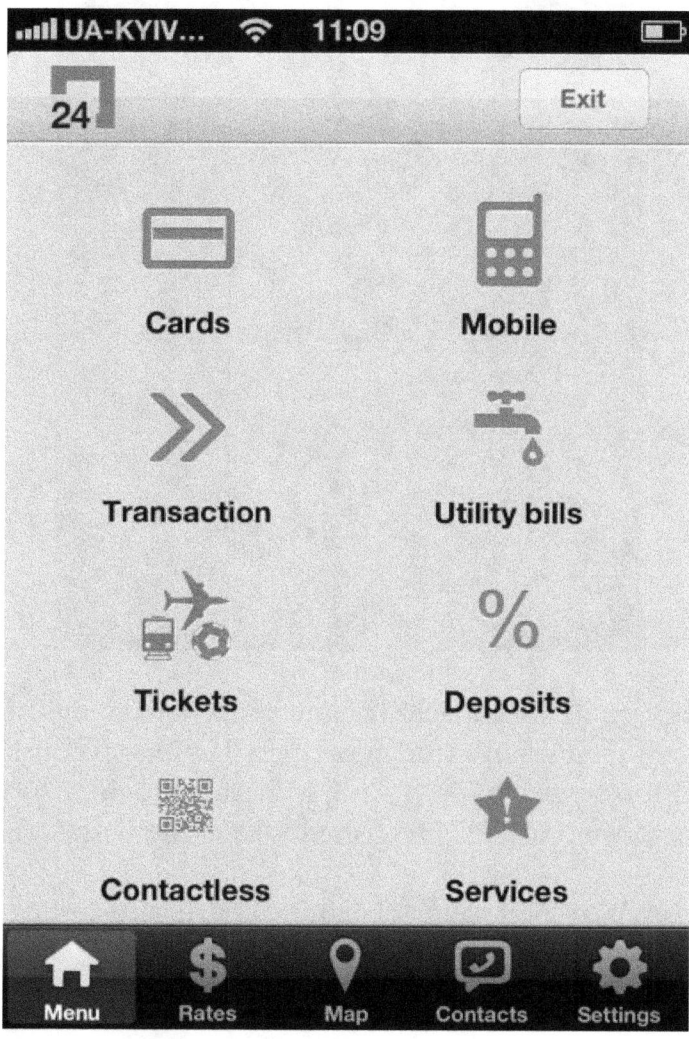

Also, this piggy bank lives in my phone. Its name is "Hryusha."

This piggy bank is connected to my personal savings account. Each time I feed it with transfers to my savings account, Hryusha looks very happy. And, if there were no incoming transfers for two weeks, Hryusha looks at me with sad eyes.

Aside from playing around, I can see charts and trends for my savings within this particular app.

Finally, I am an active user of the Evernote service and, particularly, its apps. Evernote is like an external brain, so each time I see a good discount coupon or sale, I take a picture of it and send that to Evernote with the tag "discount." That's the way I organize information so I can use it when I need to.

The major issue about using smartphones for home finances is security, not convenience or lack of choices. I do have SMS passwords for my banking app and PIN codes for other apps. It might not be the best protection; however, the benefits of using smartphones for financial purposes certainly outweigh security risks.

My security measures also include keeping an eye on my two smartphones more than on my wallet and having location tracking services, such as "Find My iPhone" activated. Google has introduced the Android Device Manager, which helps to track a lost device, as well.

The Future is Coming

I am sure that mobile devices will perform most of the home finance transactions in 5 years' time. While the usage of smartphones for analytics is limited due to small screens, the tablets are the real game-changer for analyzing personal financial data. For instance, I believe that you will be receiving all grocery-store coupons through apps and be able to import shopping data directly into your home-finances software.

I did some research on Techcrunch to find the most promising start-ups in the home-finances category. Here are the best ones I found, aside from the aforementioned LearnVest and Planwise:

Moven

Moven is a service, in which you can load, transfer, spend and track your money using your mobile device. It gives instant feedback on your spending patterns.

Also, Moven launched CRED score, the assessment of your "credibility score" (not a credit rating), which measures your financial health. It draws on a wide range of data, including your social influence, as well as answers to some finance-focused questions. Moven's CEO Brett King says, "It's not about your credit, but your credibility."

Simple

Simple calls itself the "bank of the future." It focuses on simplifying the banking process by unifying all accounts, making them accessible through your bank card.

Simple is going to introduce "Safe-to-Spend" balances within its mobile app. Rather than making money from different fees, Simple plans to split the interest margin with its partner banks. Thus, this will eliminate the incentive to push confusing products at consumers.

Unsplurge

This is a money-saving app that helps you save money in a fun way. The app is also the gateway to a community of savvy savers and spenders. Here is the quote from AppStore description: "Reach your goal! Go ahead. Buy that bag, guilt-free. Or, proudly pay off that debt. You earned it. Share with the community. Post about your success, see what everyone else is saving for, and cheer each other on. We're the support group for savvy savers."

I'm sure that there are more home-finance apps coming to the market that have social-community features and friendly support for you to reach your financial goals. Stay tuned!

Just a Few Apps Recommendations

Did you know that you can get rewards deposited directly to your PayPal by redeeming some offers within the mobile app?

iPhone users: read the wonderful article by Ruth Soukup, the author of http://www.livingwellspendingless.com called 17 Awesome Money Saving Apps.

Android users can check case study on Android apps at Stanfy's blog

Family Money Fitness Program

If you were to accomplish just one thing after reading this chapter, what would you do?

My Pick: Pick a mobile personal finance app that will bring value to you. Start using it.

P.S Good luck and might money be one thing your never argue about! Please read SUPER SUMMARY one more time!

Leo Ostapiv, Kyiv, Ukraine

www.ingramcontent.com/pod-product-compliance
Lightning Source LLC
Chambersburg PA
CBHW051329170526
45166CB00002B/735